Yadá:
To Know
and
Be Known

To Casey,
Thanks for your support!

.In Christ's love,
Kristine

Yadá:
To Know
And Be Known

Kristine Bidne

Base Twelve Publishing
Port Angeles, Washington

This book is dedicated to
my Lord and Savior Jesus Christ,
to Whom all praise, honor, glory,
and worship are due.

Life is meaningless without You.

Contents

Acknowledgments

For my Lord and Savior Jesus Christ: I'm grateful beyond words for the unconditional love, grace, mercy, forgiveness, and salvation You freely offer to me. You are my Lord, Savior, Brother, Friend. You are the Sunshine of my life, the Joy in my heart and the Air that I breathe. It's because of Your love, grace, and mercy that I have hope for the future. There is nothing I can do to make You love me any more, or less, than You do at this very moment. I know that You will never leave nor forsake me for any reason. Nothing will ever separate me from You and Your love for me, not on this day or any other, and I long for the moment I will see You face-to-face when I arrive Home. I will cheerfully spend the rest of my life expressing my love and gratitude to You in any way I can because at the end of the day, in spite of my fickle self, You will be faithful and true for all of eternity. You will always be my All in all, my Everything, my faithful Shepherd, and my Beloved. You take my breath away...and I wouldn't want it any other way.

For my dear and forbearing husband Leo, who has patiently borne the brunt of the many years I've spent learning, and am still learning, what Jesus has to teach me: While you've had many reasons over the years to throw your hands up and walk away, you've stayed by my side through thick and thin. I know there have been times I've caused you pain and frustration. I'm sorry. Please forgive me for my learning curve. Though you don't always understand me *or* my faith, you support me in my journey. For this and for so many other reasons, I love and appreciate you more than you may ever know.

For Kyle, Sarah, and David who, like your father, have borne the brunt of my many years of lessons-in-progress: I'm sorry for the mistakes I made while raising you. Please forgive me. There are so many things I wish I could go back and do over again. Changes that would have made me a better wife and mother. Choices that would have affected all of our lives for the better. But you three aren't any of those choices. You are and always will be my babies, no matter how old you are. And I will always love you more than life itself.

For my grandchildren Annella, Hannah, Benjamin, and Gabriella, who were part of the impetus for writing this book. I ache for you to personally know Jesus as your Lord and Savior. To have a living relationship with Him. And to teach that love and faith to the succeeding generations, to your children's children's children, until He returns. And for Jasmine, who is already in His loving arms.

For Marla and Fern, with whom I have laughed and cried, both in joy and agony, and ridden the turbulent waters of life: I don't know why God decided to put us together, but I will never cease to be grateful for His reasoning. Best friends don't come any better than you two, and I love you from the bottom of my heart. While we may not agree with each other on all subjects, I know we can all agree that God abundantly blessed each of us with the other two. I love you both more than I can possibly ever verbalize.

For Carla, who was such a precious part of my childhood: Over the years I wondered what you were up to and if I'd ever see you again. God must have been grinning from ear to ear when you contacted me again for the first time. I know I was. You have no idea how much joy it gave me to realize that yours was exactly the photo I needed to complete my book. I love you, my friend and sister-in-Christ, and I look forward to spending eternity with you in the presence of Papa God.

For Eileen, who once loaned me a book so I could read before going to sleep: Neither of us had a clue what was being set into motion that weekend. How different my life would have been had you not offered to let me spend the night, or if you had loaned me a different book! Thank you for being the hands, feet, and voice of Jesus. I am eternally grateful. Truly.

For Tim, who drew a line in the sand: Thank you for your Godly wisdom and leadership. May you continue to lead and guide our church for many years to come.

For Jennifer, who helped me understand yadá: You see what many don't.

For those who have encouraged me to write a book: Thank you for your kind and supportive words. Without your loving encouragement it's likely that this book never would have existed.

And finally, for my precious Mom: I've missed you terribly over the years and I long to see you when I finally arrive Home. It took me far too many years to realize that you had been God's hands and feet in action here on earth. Just about the time I finally began to mature enough to appreciate your love and wisdom, you were gone. I've always regretted that my maturity came after your passing, and that far too many of your gray hairs were probably named after me. I don't know if I ever thanked you many years ago, when I was a child, for sharing a two-page typewritten story with me that you had written. You have no idea how much, with that simple action, you inspired my writing. Thank you for your encouragement and love. I longingly look forward to our reunion in Heaven.

Introduction

The title of this book, *Yadá¹: To Know and Be Known*, is drawn from the Hebrew word yadá, which means, "To know." It's a word with multiple shades of meaning that range from head knowledge to one of extreme intimacy; from learning, perceiving, and distinguishing to becoming acquainted with, being made known, and revealing oneself.

In my ongoing journey with God, especially over the last few years, there has been an intimacy of knowing and being known that defied description until I heard the definition of yadá. My heart and soul instantly knew that yadá was *exactly* the word for which I had been searching.

While it has multiple definitions, the meaning that immediately grabbed my attention is based on relational knowledge rather than cognitive learning. When you truly yadá someone, you don't hold back. There are elements of trust, compassion, affection, passion, vulnerability, exclusivity, intimacy, and love that you share with that person. Not just head knowledge, but deep, profound heart knowledge. It's a sincere, relational knowledge that is only found when both involved parties are willing to be intimately honest and vulnerable with one other. It's the kind of relationship God yearns to have with each of us. Jeremiah 29:13 says, "You will seek me and find me when you seek me with all your heart." That, in a nutshell, is yadá. God yearns for us to truly know and be known by Him. He wants us to seek Him not only in the moments that make our souls cry out, but in every moment of every day. Every second. Every thought. Every breath.

The prayers, poems, and devotions contained within are culled from my prayer journal, which is where I go for my intimate quiet time with God. It is where I am learning to yadá Him. They mark just a few of the many peaks and valleys we have traveled during our journey together.

Each section of the book contains a different category of poetry. While some poems could have fit in multiple sections, I placed them where they seemed to make the most sense to me based on the following:

Part One - Praise and Worship: These are intended to lift up, glorify, and honor God as Father, Son, and Holy Spirit. While they're not even a drop in the bucket of what He deserves, it's a beginning.

Part Two - Guidance: These were written while seeking guidance from God in the living of day-to-day life. Some days were obviously better than others but He graciously met me in my need.

Part Three - Allegory: These contain symbolic representations of God and life. They are word-pictures that help me understand Who He is and how He has touched my life.

Part Four - Meditation: These were written during times of quiet contemplation, as I focused and meditated on God.

Part Five - Thanksgiving: Different than Section One, these were written intending to express thanks to God for Who He is and what He does.

Part Six - Love Letters From God: I've long felt that these are far less my own writing than they are taking dictation from God. Whether for me or others, these are "love letters" that I felt God putting on my heart.

Part Seven - Warfare: While God has won the war, we are still in a spiritual battle with an enemy that doesn't want to give up. These were written with those battles in mind.

Part Eight - This Doesn't Have to Be The End: This was written for anyone who longs to yadá the One Who loves them more than life itself. And yes, that means YOU!

It is my sincere prayer that, in reading this book, you will draw closer to God. That you will seek Him, yadá Him, and fall head-over-heels in love with Him. Because He's already head-over-heels in love with you.

In Christ's love,
Kristine Bidne

Part One:
Praise & Worship

"Kneeling down,
I touch Heaven itself...
as well as the heart of its King."
~ "Longing"

A Droplet of Eternity

Lord Jesus,
I can feel Your Spirit drawing near,
gently settling over me like a quilt,
pouring over me like warm honey,
filling my soul and permeating every cell.

You are the mightiest, most amazing, gracious,
merciful, compassionate, and forgiving Savior.
I could not have possibly dreamed up anything
comparable to You on my own.
My highest aspirations of what You would be like
would have fallen far short of the mark every single time.
The joy that fills my soul to overflowing, even in the midst of trials,
could only come from a gracious Creator such as You.

The time You spend with me is more precious
than all the treasures this world has to offer.
And the thought of spending eternity with You?
My mind cannot wrap around it, yet I long for the moment it begins.
After only a taste; a sip; a mere droplet of Your glory and Presence,
I have longed for that day ever since...
the moment I will enter into Your presence forever.
Nothing this world has to offer can compare.

It's been over twenty years, yet I feel as if it was yesterday.
My soul will never forget how You
poured Your Spirit into this cracked, inadequate vessel.
The absolute, stark, overpowering knowledge that I was so very
naked and vulnerable in Your Presence.
Every sin I had ever committed was laid bare.
I had nowhere to hide. From You. From my sin. From myself.
And yet just as absolute, stark, and overpowering
was the Love You poured over me.
I have never felt more loved, before or since.

It was as if a tidal wave washed over me.
A tsunami.
I was so very naked.
So very vulnerable.
And so very, very loved.
Is it any wonder that it felt as if my heart and soul exploded?
Literally warming me
from my soul to the tips of my fingers and toes?
It was just a moment. A sip of Your glory. A taste. A droplet.
I have spent, and will spend, the rest of my life longing
for the moment I will be with You face-to-face.

For if that was a mere droplet,
what of eternity?

You undo me, Lord, in ways that mere words
cannot even begin to convey.
I know that I am a work-in-progress.
I know I have a lifetime to go before I will be who You designed me to be.
I know that I will spend the rest of my life trying to be that person.
And I know that it will only be through Your strength, mercy, forgiveness,
love, and compassion that I will ever turn into that woman.

Yet I also know that I will cheerfully, willingly, gratefully spend
the rest of my life letting You mold and shape me into Your image.
It doesn't always feel good, and sometimes You scare me,
but I find myself looking forward to the end results.
Because regardless of what happens, I love and trust You.
For I know You will never leave nor forsake me.
I know I can trust whatever plan it is that You have for me.
Because in the middle of it all I'll still be in the palm of Your hand.
And there is nowhere I would rather be.

I give You all of me,
as well as all glory, honor, praise, and worship.

Forever.

Pure Worship

It's just You and me, Lord.

I see through a glass darkly, [2]
but You don't.

You see through my pretenses and facades.
You know which gifts of worship I offer to You are real
and which are beautifully wrapped, empty packages.

You know the true cost of each gift,
as well as whether or not my "sacrifice" is re-gifted
because I no longer want it.

I long to bring You a sweet-smelling first-fruit offering,
not a decaying afterthought of crumbs that dishonor You.

You don't want a beautiful, empty song
anymore than You would want that beautiful, empty package.

You know whether or not my worship is truly from my heart,
and if any sacrifice was involved on my part.

You know whether true change is taking place
or if I'm just wrapping more empty packages.

Lord, I seek to honor and glorify You with everything I am.
No reserved corners. No facades. No empty packages.
I long to give my best to the One who gave me His all.
To worship You not just with song, praise, and prayers
but with my life.

I choose to open my life and lay it down on Your altar,
giving all of myself to the One who gave me Everything.

I no longer want to give you empty words and gestures,
or an empty heart and soul.
Please forgive me, Lord,
for You are worthy of
all glory, honor, praise and worship for all of eternity.
Pure worship, not a cheap imitation.

At the end of my life,
having given You the purest worship possible,
I will fall far short of the mark of giving You Your due.
You already know that.
But in Your gracious love, mercy, and compassion,
You accept my gifts as though they were priceless jewels.
You don't ask for perfection...You simply ask for my best effort.

I am utterly undone before You.

Naked. Vulnerable.
Pathetic in my humanity.
Yet You love me with a passion I cannot comprehend.

And so I offer You all of me.
Heart.
Soul.
Mind.
Life.

It's not much.
It's small, and it's broken, but it's all of me.
I offer it up to You as a living sacrifice,
to do with as You will.

Help me to honor You as You deserve:
with every single breath of my life.

All for You
and for Your glory.

My Heavenly Father

Father God,
You truly are a good Father.

My earthly father didn't always have my best interest at heart.
There were trust issues for good reasons.

But You, O Lord, are the perfect Father.

I may not always understand or agree with Your plans for my life
but I know that I can always trust You,
and trust that You have my best interest at heart.

When I wander far from You and cannot see You
for the darkness that surrounds me,
Your Holy Spirit urgently calls out to me,
warning me of my dangerous path.
Your voice guides me Home.

In times of trouble, I can run to You and pour my heart out.
You gather me in Your arms and comfort me,
gently chastising me when necessary,
but You always discipline me in love.

Nothing can compare with the peace and joy
that pour over me in waves,
the approval from Your Spirit to mine,
when I am walking close to You.
Nothing.

It is a gift in and of itself.

The sacrifices that You made
so that I could have this relationship with You
stupefy and humble me...because I know myself.

I know what You had to work with during some of my lowest points.
Even now.

And the fact that You chose to make those sacrifices
just so I could have the opportunity to be part of Your family
overwhelms and undoes me.

Completely.

Utterly.

I find my spirit down on the floor in front of You.
Humbled. Sobbing. Grateful.

Because You are a good Father Who loves His children so very much.
Even the prodigals.

Thank You, Father God;
my Abba.

Thank You, Lord Jesus;
my Savior.

Thank You, Holy Spirit;
my Comforter and my Guide.

Thank You for adopting this wayward child into Your family.

Now and forevermore.

I Am Yours

I can't help but look back at our journey as we've traveled together.
How much You loved me before I even loved You...
more than life itself. [3.]

How You called me in from the darkness
and welcomed me back when I wandered away from You. [4.]

How faithful You have been in spite of my unfaithfulness,
for You cannot deny Yourself. [5.]

How much You've taught, supported, strengthened, and blessed me
through the indwelling of the Holy Spirit. [6.]

I cannot help but look forward to our continuing journey,
knowing You will be right by my side. [7.]

You truly are the Christ, the Messiah,
and my only hope of salvation. [8.]

Your ways, while confusing to me at times,
are truly perfect and mighty. [9.]

Your love knows no bounds,
for Your love has no boundaries. [10.]

Your blessings are without restraint,
for You are a Father Who knows what His children need. [11.]

Your grace is beautiful beyond comprehension,
and freely given with an open hand. [12.]

Your mercy is more precious than all the treasures
that this world can offer. [13.]

Your forgiveness is without measure,
in spite of my unrighteousness. [14.]

No one deserves the abundance You've bestowed upon me.
No one.
Yet You bestow it freely, generously, unreservedly.[15.]

You give in ways I cannot understand,
for reasons beyond my comprehension. [16.]

Time and time again You have welcomed me back with open arms
when I have turned away from You. [17.]

You truly are a good Father in all Your ways.

May all glory, honor, praise and worship be Yours,
for You truly are the only One worthy of it.

Thank You, Father God.
Thank You, Lord Jesus.
Thank You, Holy Spirit.

I offer myself fully to You and to Your service.
Use me.

Let me be Your hands, feet, and voice in this sin-stained world.
Let me be Your bond-servant.
Please.

I offer my ear to the post, Lord.
Mark me.

For I am Yours.

Homesick

Lord Jesus,
I am so very undone by Your Presence.

Out of the corner of my eye
I saw a reflection
of the faintest flicker of Your glory.
I cannot fathom the magnitude of Your full glory
when just that mere sidelong glimpse wreaked me completely.

And yet...
I long for the day I will see You face-to-face.

Like a child waiting eagerly for her beloved Daddy to come home,
I long to run into Your arms and be welcomed by Your loving embrace.

My soul cries out for You, knowing that all is not right
when I am not physically in Your presence.

I am Homesick, Lord.
Truly Homesick.

My soul aches for You.
Not because things are going badly,
but because You are so very good.

You are mighty, gracious, compassionate, and loving
in ways I can neither count nor fathom.

Your ways are beyond my comprehension,
yet I cannot help but trust You with my heart, soul, and life.

The crumbs from Your table
would nourish me beyond measure,
but You don't expect me to survive on the crumbs.

Instead, You adopted me and gave me full access to Your table.
Lush, rich, Spirit-filled nourishment that satiates my soul
and overflows to those around me.
You've lifted me up to grace, love, and faith that I never knew existed.
You've helped me realize how many years I wasted
chasing my own dreams instead of Yours,
yet You do not hold my folly against me.

Instead You lovingly draw me
into a closer relationship with You.

Thank You, my Lord.

For accepting and loving this perpetually wayward child.
For calling me Yours.
For allowing me to call You mine.

I long for the day I will be part
of the countless multitude at the end of days,
lifting Your Name up on high, praising, worshiping,
and glorifying You as only You deserve.

To You be all glory, worship, honor, and praise.

Now and forevermore.

But God...

But God...

...died for me, my family, and the whole world. Once for all.

...is right beside me as well as inside me.

...has plans for me.
His plans are perfect, and more important than those of anyone else.
Even my own.

...can help me push the boulders in life.

...is my Lord; Master; Savior; Friend.

...thinks more of a sacrificial heart than the sacrifice.

...knows me inside and out, and loves me anyway.

...is more than enough.

...is able; at all times and in all ways.

...is merciful, faithful, and compassionate.

...is there when everyone else falls away.

...will never leave me nor forsake me. Ever.

...is more than I can imagine or comprehend.

...gives me strength when I am weak.

...is The Alpha and Omega. The Beginning and The End. Eternal.

...is the Great I Am.

...formed me in my mother's womb.

...conquered sin and death.

...is all-knowing, all-seeing, and ever-present.

...is, was, and always will be.

...will never say, "I didn't see that coming."

...cannot deny Himself.

...longs to be in relationship with me.

...is tender, merciful, gracious, compassionate, and forgiving.

...is faithful and just.

...keeps His promises.

...is molding and shaping me into His image.
It's a lifelong process, but the end results will be worth it.

...welcomes me back with open arms when I have been His prodigal child.

...will never say, "That's a sin I can't forgive."

...does not limit His love, forgiveness, compassion, mercy, and grace.

...is worth more than any treasure this world has to offer.

...is always available, no matter the hour. No matter the crisis.

...helps me to remember, when the enemy tries to deceive me,
"But God..."

Running to Your Arms

Lord Jesus,
You undo me in ways I can neither count nor fathom.
I am completely and utterly undone.

Running to Your arms,
I feel my heart, my soul, and my walls crumbling.

I am in tears.

Overwhelmed by waves of Your Spirit pouring down on me,
I feel as though I've gone underwater in the deep end of the pool.
I can neither touch the bottom, nor can I rise above the surface.
I am completely submerged and devastated before Your presence.

But there is nowhere else I would rather be.

I long to stay here, in Your presence.
I yearn for the day I will see You face-to-face,
able to worship You for eternity as You deserve.

Thank You for Your grace, mercy, love, forgiveness, and Spirit.
You are mighty in all of Your ways,
and I live to worship You.

Longing

Longing
for the day that my heart
will match Yours beat for beat.

Listening
for the breath of Your Spirit,
my soul quieting as it washes over me.

Loving
the Master that sought me out and saved me
in spite of myself.

Lifting
my life, my soul, and my spirit up to You,
knowing that they are in good Hands.

Bowing
down to lay them at Your feet,
wishing that I could offer You more.

Offering
You all that I was, am, and ever will be
on the altar of my heart and soul.

A living sacrifice for a living God.

Kneeling down,
I touch Heaven itself...
as well as the heart of its King.

Undone

Lord, Lord...
and at that, I find myself speechless; words fail me.
Not out of any sense of despair, but out of gratitude, love, joy, awe, and fear.
Good fear.
Such a deep, profound sense of respect and worship that my mind
and mouth cannot form the words to express my thoughts and feelings.
Instead, the Holy Spirit must translate my spiritual groanings
as my soul lays prostrate before You.

I am undone in Your Presence.

I am overwhelmed by Your grace, mercy, peace, forgiveness, and love.
My spirit and soul long for the day that I am rid of this mortal shell
and I can stand, kneel, or fall flat on my face in Your Presence
and do nothing but praise, worship, and glorify You for all eternity.
For You are a holy and righteous King, worthy of all glory, honor and praise.
You hem me in on all sides.
You know my every thought, desire, and deed.
Every want and need that I have here on earth
is nothing but a poor substitute for what I truly want: You.
I long to drink in the Light of Your Spirit.
To nourish my soul with Your eternal words.
To clothe myself in Your eternal righteousness, grace, mercy, and love.
To shelter myself under Your wings.
To lift up my hands, fall on my knees, and seek Your face.
All for, and because of, Your glory.
You are the Light in Whom there is no darkness.
The Living Water that quenches true thirst.
The Bread of Life that nourishes the soul.
A Shelter in time of need.
I ache for the day I will see You face-to-face.
While looking forward to the day
the desires of my heart and soul will truly be fulfilled,
I pray this in Your precious and holy Name... Amen.

Transformed

Lord Jesus.
Master.
Redeemer.
Beloved Savior.

I am so completely undone before You.

Tears.
Joyfully devastated.
Loved.

I went from...
Unworthy to accepted.
Sinner to forgiven.
Prodigal to heiress.
Pauper to princess.
Damned to redeemed.

I love You so very much,
my precious Lord.

Thank You for all You've done,
are doing,
and ever will do.

You are amazing.

I live to worship You.

Names and Attributes

Lord Jesus. Savior. Master. Friend. Abba. Comforter.
Alpha and Omega. Merciful God. Mighty and Righteous Judge.
Healer. My One True Love. Yahweh. Yeshua. Redeemer.
Lover of my Soul. Lion of Judah. Lamb of God.
King of Kings. Lord of Lords.

Thank You...
For Your gracious, overflowing, abundant, merciful love.
For the abundant blessings You have showered upon us.
Kindness. Compassion. Joy. Mercy. Forgiveness. Salvation. Love. Grace.
The list goes on and on, Lord.

I lift You and Your Name up in praise, glory and worship.
You alone are worthy. Mighty. Gracious.
You alone are the One Who can lift my head and tell me to rise,
for You alone have saved me.
I did, and can do, nothing to deserve such grace and mercy,
yet You lavish them upon me regardless.
You are my Everything, Lord, and I bow down and worship You.
You are mighty in all of Your ways,
and faithful in ways I cannot even begin to comprehend.
Like a swollen, raging river, Your mercy overflows all boundaries.
Like raw honey from the comb, Your love is sweet, rich,
life-giving, healing, and nourishing.
Like a pardon extended to a lifelong, hardened criminal on Death Row,
Your forgiveness is undeserved and bountiful,

You are more than I ever dreamed possible, Lord.
Order my steps throughout this day
that I may honor, worship, and glorify You in all that I say and do.
Help me to be a beacon that shines toward You,
that others may see what a gracious, loving God You are.
Help me to die to self daily, that others may live.
For You alone.

Joyfully Devastated

Lord God. Maker of Heaven and earth. Alpha and Omega.
Emmanuel. King of Kings. Lord of Lords.
Infinite. Omnipotent. Omniscient.
Yahweh. Lion of Judah. The Lamb That Was Slain.
Chief Shepherd. Healer. Rabbi. My One True Love.

I could go on naming Your Names and Your attributes
until this and many more books were full to overflowing.
In the end, I would run out of paper and ink
before I could run out of praise, honor, and glory
for You and Your tender mercies.

I am reminded of the day I was filled with Your Holy Spirit.
Even remembering it I am joyfully devastated,
wanting to bow down at Your feet,
worshiping You with all and everything in me.
That day I caught only the slightest glimpse of Your glory,
nothing more than the merest reflection out of the corner of one eye,
yet I was completely and thoroughly undone.
I cannot fathom being able to withstand the fullness of Your glory.
Lord, please forgive me for trying to make You small enough
that my finite mind could wrap around Your magnitude.
You are unfathomable yet You draw near and bend down,
that I may come near and rest in the shadow of Your wings.

Once again, I am undone.
Joyfully devastated by Your nearness.
Humbled by the lavish love You pour over me.
Awestruck by the priceless Treasure that You are.
Breathless. Grateful. Amazed.

Thank You, Lord Jesus.
I lift up and glorify You and Your holy, righteous Name,
now and forevermore.

Your Very Nature

You have no rival, my Lord.
From the beginning of time until the end of days,
You alone are mighty.

You alone are worthy of all praise, glory, and honor.

Your ways exceed my wildest imagination.
Your thoughts surpass my deepest contemplation.

You set the universe in motion,
yet You still loved me enough to die in my place.

Your grace, mercy, love, and forgiveness know no bounds,
and Your joy over each lost sheep that is rescued
is a thing of beauty.

Your faithfulness is incomparable
and Your compassion has no equal.

There is nothing I have done, or ever will do,
that warrants such unmitigated love.
Such endless grace and mercy.

Your very nature shines through bright and clear,
and Your love seeps into my very soul.

It is...
simply and succinctly...
You.

Blessed are You, Lord!

May your Name be glorified at all times and in all ways!
Now and forevermore!

Great Physician

Lord, I praise You in the middle of my physical problems
because I know that You are the Great Physician.
I know that one day I will be with You
and there will be no more sickness, pain, or tears.
I know that You are mighty in all of Your ways
yet You are gentle of heart, filled with love and compassion.

In my wildest dreams
I could never have imagined such a Savior,
nor could I have imagine how much You would
love and care for this cracked, leaky vessel.

But I don't have to imagine it,
because the truth far surpasses my wildest dreams.

For here You are.
And here I am.

Thank You, Lord.
For everything.

You have blessed me in ways I cannot fathom for Your own purposes.
I may not understand Your plans, but they are perfect in all of their ways.

You are a mighty, righteous, and compassionate God,
and I praise and thank You from the bottom of my heart and soul.

Please open my eyes, ears, heart and soul to Your will.
Let me be Your hands, feet, and voice in whatever way You need.

I am Your grateful bond-servant,
and I live to worship, honor, and glorify You.

Father God

Father God.
Two words.
So seemingly incongruous,
yet so inexplicably interwoven.

They are so confusing to the world at large,
yet so right to the ones that know You.

Giving. Loving. Guiding.
Omnipotent. Omniscient. Omnipresent.
Provider. Sustainer. Protector.
Merciful. Faithful. Wonderful.
Forgiving. Gracious. Love.

Words alone cannot describe You.
They fail miserably, falling far short of Who You truly are.

Your faithfulness knows no bounds,
even in the midst of our faithlessness.

Your love cannot be measured,
for so great a measurement does not exist.

Your mercy has no equal.
Your forgiveness is as endless as it is bountiful.

Your grace is unparalleled. Your peace is unforgettable.

You truly are our Abba Adonai.
Beloved Father.
Beloved God.
Beloved Lord and Master.
Beloved.
And so much more.

Eternal

You are magnificent, Lord.

Glorious beyond my wildest imagination.
Compassionate beyond expectation.
Loving beyond measure.
Righteous in all of Your ways.
Faithful to the faithless.
Forgiving to the unforgivable.

No one compares to You, Lord.

I could praise You from now til the end of time
and there would still be praise left unsaid.
Glory left unstated.

Great
is the Name of the God of Abraham, Isaac and Jacob!

Mighty
is He Who was always there before the beginning of time
and Who will always be there after the end of time!

Glorious
is He Who spoke the universe into being
and Who will roll the stars back like a scroll!

Righteous
is He to Whom all knees will bow,
and to Whom all tongues will confess
that Jesus Christ is Lord!

Honorable
is He Who judges all!

Blessed is the Name of the Lord!

Your Handiwork

Thank You, Lord, for the beauty of this day.

For even amidst this cloudy, rainy, breezy day
the evidence of Your handiwork is staggeringly obvious.

Without the clouds the rain could not fall.

Without the rain all life would wither and dry up,
scattering like so much dust in the desert.

Without the breeze
the air would become stagnant, heavy, and putrid.

The intricacy of a single leaf;
the ephemeral wisp of a passing cloud;
the complexity of a drop of dew lying gently on a blade of grass;
all point toward the Hands of a gracious, thoughtful, loving God.
A divine Creator who thoughtfully crafted each and every
atom, neutron, neuron, cell, building block and form of life in existence.

As much as any artist is known by their body of work,
whether they sign their masterpieces or not,
the work of Your hands can be seen all around us.

Your signature is self-evident for those who take the time
to look, appreciate, and glorify
the handiwork of the Master.

Nothing and Everything

Nothing I can do, say, or believe,
other than the righteousness of Jesus Christ,
will ever make me more, or less, acceptable before You,
my Heavenly Father.

Nothing I've ever done, and nothing I will ever do,
can make me better, or worse, in Your eyes than I am at this moment.
I am eternally loved and accepted.

My salvation isn't dependent on my works in any way, shape, or form.
I simply seek to honor and glorify the One Who loved me first.

Though You could dismiss me as worthless,
You treasure me.

You say that You are my Beloved
and that I am Yours.

You allow me to add my nothing to Your everything.
You fill in the gaps as Your Spirit continues to move in my life,
changing, molding, and shaping me into Your image
until the day I stand before You, transformed.
Complete.

Though I can give You nothing,
I owe You everything,
for You are Everything to me.

Now and forevermore.

As Your Spirit Settles

I feel an overwhelming sense of peace, joy, and Your presence
settling gently down on me like a sheet.

Which sounds completely unimpressive without the context.

As a child I used to pull my top bed sheet up,
way up, as far as I could reach,
then quickly pull the top of it back down again.
The bottom of the sheet, tucked under the mattress,
would create an air pocket
and the sheet would billow out like a parachute.
The air captured inside would pour out like a wave,
rushing over my body and bathing me in its coolness.
Then, as the sheet settled, it would gently work its way
into all the nooks, crannies and crevices,
bringing a gentle caress wherever it touched.
With childish glee
I would do it over and over again.

From the rush of air to the gentle caress as it falls into place,
as well as my own childlike joy and anticipation,
this reminds me of Your Spirit as it
blows like a gentle breeze across my soul,
washing over and settling on me,
bringing a gentle caress wherever It touches.

Thank You, Lord, for the gentle touch of Your Spirit,
for leaving Your Comforter until Your return,
and for such a priceless,
magnificent Gift.

No Higher Reward

Lord, even as my body was still waking up this morning,
my soul turned toward You and smiled...because it knew.

Knew...
That You are the One that truly makes me complete.
That You are the righteous and mighty Creator, Judge, and Savior of all.
That my time here on earth may seem an eternity, but it's not.
That a moment will come when my soul's eternity will truly begin.
That it will be an eternity centered on praising and worshiping You.

And I'm looking forward to that moment with every fiber of my being.

Lord Jesus, I cannot help but lift my hands up to You in praise and worship.
You are mighty. Righteous. Glorious. The Beginning and the End.
My Savior. Brother. Friend. Life-Giver. Lord. Master. King.
You are beautiful, loving, compassionate,
faithful, gentle, forgiving, and merciful.

You are the apple of my eye,
the joy in my heart,
the air that I breath,
and the wind beneath my wings.
You are my Lord, my Shepherd, my Beloved, my Everything,
and I love You more than life itself.

As the deer pants for the water, Lord, [18.]
so my soul longs for You.
Help me to be the disciple You intended me to be,
that I may honor You in all that I say and do.

For I long to hear You say to me,
"Well done, good and faithful servant."

There could truly be no higher reward.

You

You are so much more than I can fathom.
My mind wants to put You into neat, tidy boxes,
organized and compartmentalized.

But You cannot and will not be contained by such small-thinking.

You...
Who created the heavens and the earth.

You...
Who command the armies of Heaven.

You...
Who knit me together in my mother's womb.

You...
Righteous Judge Who paid my penalty with Your life,
then came back and razed hell.

You...
Whose love cannot be measured.

You...
The avenging, righteous Redeemer guarding His sheep.

You...
Lord.
Savior.
Master.
Brother.
Friend.

My problems don't stand a chance against The Great I Am...
You.

To Know You Better

It occurs to me, Lord, how very often I come to You to talk,
bare my soul, and ask for Your help,
all without stopping to ask how You are.

You are the Almighty, the Alpha and Omega, the One True God.
You are my Master, Savior, King, Brother, Friend.
You are All-knowing, All-Seeing, All-Powerful, Always Present.
These are just a few of Your Names and attributes,
and all are completely true.

While it may seem a silly thing to ask,
I cannot help but wonder...how are You this morning, Lord?

You know what will happen until the end of time,
but does Your heart break over what the human race has done
to Your beautiful Creation and to each other?

You know the very moment when You will say, "Enough!",
but does Your anger burn and spill over at the atrocities You see?

Though none are a surprise to You,
do You weep over our failures and rejoice over our successes?

Do You have Someone in whom You confide?

Lord, You know my heart.
I ask none of this in jest or rancor, but simple love and concern
for a Master Who loved me more than life itself,
as well as a deep desire to know You as You know me.

I love You.

In Your merciful Name I seek Your face and pray...
Amen.

Your Plans

I don't know what plans You have for me, Lord.
I don't even know what tomorrow will bring.

But in spite of that, maybe even because of it,
I say with every fiber of my being
that You are my King, Lord, Savior, Brother, Master, and Friend,
and that, come what may, I love and trust You.

Even though You've had ample reasons to reject me, You haven't.
You came alongside me and loved me in spite of myself.
In spite of my faults and weaknesses,
You forgave my sins and accepted me as Your own,
engulfing me in a flood of love that I never even knew existed.

Thank You.
For all of that and so much more.

For Your faithfulness in spite of my betrayal.
For drawing me close to You.
For being my Kinsman Redeemer.
For the blessings and answers to prayer that I know about...
and for the ones that I don't.

You are beautiful in ways I cannot even begin to describe.
Instead, the Holy Spirit must translate my thoughts and groanings.

Thank You for Your gracious mercy, Lord.
Mercy so great that my brain refuses to wrap around it.

I lift my hands up to You and praise Your glorious Name
and thank You for Your enduring compassion.

In Your precious and holy Name I pray...
Amen.

Good Morning, Lord

As I woke up this morning, my soul turning toward You,
whispering, 'Good morning, Lord!',
I couldn't help but smile.

For though I am far from perfect,
You long to hear from me.

The fact that You seek me out....
wanting to be in relationship with me,
wanting me to be in relationship with You,
meeting me when I draw near to You,
...will never grow old.

Though only half-awake,
I could feel Your gentle smile,
Your love,
and the warmth of Your nearby Presence in my soul.

I never cease to wonder at the joy and peace that surround You,
or that You extend it to me even in the midst of a storm.

You are wonderful and beautiful beyond words,
and I cannot ever thank You enough for loving me in spite of myself.

All that I have, and all that I am,
I give back to You with open hands.
Use it as You will, for I love and trust You.

Do you scare me at times?
Oh, yes.

But my love and trust for You far outweigh my fears,
for You are my faithful Shepherd, Redeemer, and Beloved.

Part Two: Guidance

"Show me the Way You have laid out for me
and help me to stay on Your path..."
~ *"Hot Mess"*

Face-to-Face

Lord Jesus, I cannot help but wonder what I would say
if You were sitting face-to-face with me.

What would be on my heart to tell You?

Yet prayer is nothing more than my heart and soul
having a conversation with their Creator.
So, Lord, I come to You with what is on my heart today:

I'm sorry I haven't been all You designed me to be.
The last thing I've ever wanted to do was disappoint You,
yet sometimes it seems like that must be all that I ever do.
My heart and soul ache to serve You, and serve You well,
yet my flesh is traitorous to the bone.
I'm so very sorry.
Please forgive me and give me Your strength
and wisdom to do Your will.

I need You.
Not just every day, but every hour; minute; second; nanosecond.
Not a moment of my life goes by that I don't need Your saving grace,
Your boundless mercy, and Your endless love.
As much as I need the air that I breathe, I need You more.
Because I am far too human for my own good.
My only hope for change is the infiltration of my soul by Your Spirit.
I cannot be trusted, on my own, to do what is right.
Without You, without Your Spirit, I am morally and spiritually bankrupt.
Please help me. I beg of You.

There may be times when I give up on myself in frustration and defeat,
but I know that You will never give up on me.
You will keep coming back for me, time and time again,
until I understand my true value in You.
And even after that, when I stumble and fall,

You will be there for me until and throughout eternity.

While I am not worthy to look into them,
I lose myself when I look into Your eyes.
I am completely undone.
From them I see Your love and compassion shining clear and strong.
Time seems to slow to a standstill
as I free-fall under Your gaze of mercy and grace.
Words fail me, tears of joy and gratitude flow unchecked.

You take my breath away.

I hear when You whisper to me.
In the morning, afternoon, evening; even in the dead of night.
Sometimes the noise of this world tries to drown You out,
and I don't always answer You when I should,
but I hear the still, small whisper of Your Spirit to mine.

I know that while I have ached for You and Your Presence,
You have ached for me and mine more.
That is not intended to be egotistical...
it's simply an acknowledgment
that in loving me enough to die in my place,
You paid the ultimate price to be close to me for all of eternity.
But by not answering You,
by not drawing near to You,
I negate the reason You sacrificed Yourself for me.
Please forgive me, Lord, for my selfishness.
For breaking Your heart.
For the tears You've wept over me.

Help me, Lord.
To honor You.
To lift up and glorify Your Name.
To always hear and respond to the call of Your voice.
To sing over You as You sing over me.
Now and forevermore.

Offerings

Do my offerings to You reveal what I truly believe about You?

Lord God.
My Savior.
My Redeemer.
My Friend.

The above thought cuts me to the heart.
As it should.

You have loved me wholeheartedly.
Selflessly.
Completely.

In spite of myself.

I've lifted my hands up to Heaven,
proclaiming my undying love for You,
all while keeping the first fruits for myself
and giving you the pathetic, rotting remnants.

Lord Jesus.
Father God.
Precious Spirit.
Please forgive me.

Though I have come a long way,
and that only because of You, Your love, and Your strength,
times like this show me I have so much further to go!

The enemy would have me believe it is impossible,
or that I am unforgivable, but in You neither is true.
I throw myself down at Your feet and on Your great mercy,
seeking Your forgiveness as well as Your help and guidance.

I cannot "get there" on my own, Lord.

But You do not require that.
You only require that I have a willing heart.
One willing to let You be its Lord and Master,
allowing You to lead, and willing to follow You.

Lord, I offer You my whole heart.
It is small, slightly hardened,
and it has a bad habit of being selfish.

Teach it to soften and grow, Lord.
Teach it to encompass Your will.
Show it Your possibilities.
Teach it to not be so selfish and small-minded.
Teach it to love as You do.

Help me in my unbelief, Lord,
that I may be the disciple You created me to be.
The disciple I long to be.
Help others to see that the only reason I changed was You,
and give them a thirst for Your change in their own lives.

All for,
and because of,
Your glory.

In Your precious, priceless Name I pray...
Amen.

Hot Mess

Lord, please help me.
I'm such a hot mess, and You're the only One who can fix me.

There is no valid reason why You should,
except that You are a gracious, loving, merciful God.

One that keeps the promises He makes.
One that is faithful despite my faithlessness.
One that extends forgiveness, over and over again,
to this exceedingly broken, ungrateful child.
I deserve to see nothing but the back of You
striding purposefully away from me.
And yet, over and over again, I look up
to see You running toward me,
arms held open wide as You welcome me home.

I don't deserve You.

I don't deserve Your love.
I don't deserve Your grace, mercy, and forgiveness.
And therein lies the rub of the truth:
that while I don't deserve any of it, You freely offer it to me.
It is mine to receive.
All I need to do is reach out my hands, open them,
and accept the free gifts You are offering me.

So why do I falter? Why do I doubt?

It's possible I let my fears and pride get in the way.
Or perhaps I've been listening too closely
to the enemy's whispers of guilt and shame.

Whatever the reason, the result is the same:
a faltering doubt that creeps into my walk with You.

I cannot help but think of others and wonder their reasons.

Some simply cannot accept Your love.
Like a feral animal, they circle warily,
growling, sniffing, suspicious, agitated,
recoiling in fear at the mere suggestion of Your touch.

Others cower in fear, paralyzed.
Unable to ever remember a kind word or touch,
they have no reference for comparison.
So they hunker down to protect themselves.

Still others refuse to trust because it would mean
giving control of their lives over to an unknown Quantity;
they'd rather take their chances on their own mistakes,
unaware of the freedom and life they lose by doing so.

Where do I lie on that spectrum, Lord?

I know Your love, grace, mercy, and compassion.
I've felt and seen them in action.
Yet still I cower.
Disobey.
Make poor choices.
Refuse Your gifts.
Try to remain in control of my life.

Lord, please help me.
To draw near to You instead of wandering away.
To seek You and Your face, Your heart, and Your approval.
To open my heart and my hands to Your gifts.
To trust You enough to accept Your will, come what may.

Show me the Way You have laid out for me
and help me to stay on Your path.

All for the sake of Your holy, righteous, matchless Name,

Search Me, O God

Search me, O God, and know my heart... [19.]
Father God, You created me.
You know every part of me from the inside out.
Every cell, every pore, every hair, every bone.
Even my soul.
As ephemeral and invisible as it is, You know my heart and soul.
I open it up to You for examination, Lord.
Every nook and cranny.
Every spot I've reserved for myself.
I open them all and give You free access.
Search me, Lord.
Search my innermost being as only You can.

...Test me and know my anxious thoughts...
Lord, as I sit here trying to meditate and focus on You,
I find myself distracted by minutiae.
Things that don't normally bother me are interfering.
The noise of the fridge, the streetlight outside, the temperature of the room.
After minimizing the distractions, I still find my attention wandering
because the distraction is white noise that is coming from within myself.
Daily concerns that are rumbling along at a low-level,
but when added together they become noisy enough to interfere.

Test me, Lord.

Send out spiritual sonar to flesh out the anxious thoughts.
Show me the dangers that lurk beneath the surface, trying to interfere.
I give these anxious thoughts over to You,
for 'Who of you by worrying can add a single hour to his life'? [20.]
Thank You for the peace washing over me in giving them to You.
Please keep testing me, my Lord, that these anxious thoughts may be brought
captive from out of the darkness and into the Light,
exposing them for what they are:
distractions sent by the enemy in order to interfere.

See if there is any offensive way in me...
Lord, I long to hear You say,
"Well done, good and faithful servant." [21.]
Yet I know there are ways of mine
that could cause me not to hear You say that.
I offer those ways up to You as a pleasing sacrifice,
for it is You and Your opinion that truly matter to me.
Everything else, no matter how good or pleasing,
no matter how tempting,
is nothing more than a distraction from You.
Everything.

Help me in my unbelief, Lord, for I am a weak, fallible child.
Yet I yearn to please and serve You, my gracious Master.

...and lead me in the Way everlasting...
Lord, You are the One True God.
You are *the* Way, *the* Truth, and *the* Light...
there is no way to the Father but by You.
Please lead me in Your Way,
teaching me what You want me to learn,
that I may come alongside others and be a beacon to You.
Keep my heart soft, Lord,
that my feet will naturally stay on Your path.
Illuminate weaknesses in me,
that I may offer them up to You as a sacrifice.

I love You more than I know how to express.
Help me to live in such a way that my love for You is obvious to others,
and they can't help but be drawn to You because of it.

My precious Lord.
Savior. Redeemer. Friend.
Search me, O God,
and know my heart.

As only You can.

Dross and Gold

Lord Jesus, You are my only Hope
that I will ever be more gold than dross.

I long to hear You say, "Well done, good and faithful servant."
I continue to lean on You and Your strength,
praying that one day I will hear you say those words to me.

I need You.
For so many, many reasons,
but also because I cannot do this on my own.

I am a weak, fallible human being whose flesh has its own agenda.
I am learning from my journey with You, and my trials,
but I still have so much more to learn.

Sometimes I think You must throw Your hands up in the air,
despairing that I will ever learn,
but I know that's the enemy's voice hissing at me.
So with You at my side, I ignore him and continue on.

I choose to keep leaning on You and Your strength.

It will never be by my own strength
that purification will come to pass;
only by Your strength.

Please help me in my unbelief, beloved Savior.

Help me to be the disciple and steward that You want me to be.
That I yearn to be.

Turn me from dross to gold, my Lord, that I may shine for You.

Now and for all of eternity.

Wonder-struck

Help me to look through Your eyes, Lord.
Keep my awareness of the Wonder that is You at a high level.
Help me to focus on You, Your Word, and Your daily blessings.
Reveal more and more of Your heart to me and teach me
to seek You out wherever You show up in my day.

For while my faith is more than just emotions,
I love hearing from You and feeling You near.
I love to see Your hands and heart at work around me.
From the beauty and artistry of Your creations
to the tender mercies You offer us daily.
From the kiss of the sun on the horizon
to the thunder of the ocean's roar.
From the miracle of life, both finite and infinite,
to the stirring of Your Spirit in my soul.
From the bittersweet beauty of Your death
to the shouts of acclamation at Your resurrection.
From the love, grace, and compassion that burst Heaven's boundaries
and pour down on me like a waterfall
to Your soon and coming return.

Open my eyes to the wonder You have strewn about me.
Like a small child whose eyes light up at each new discovery,
let my heart and soul abound in continual amazement
at the ways Your grace, compassion, love, mercy, and tenderness
are extended to me each and every day.
At the whisper of Your Spirit to mine.
Fill me to overflowing with Your wonder, Lord,
that the praises of my heart and soul may flow back to You.
Keep me wonder-struck,
that I may never tire of the Wonder that is You.

In Your precious, mighty, and righteous Name I pray...
Amen.

Missing You

Father God, earlier today I was annoyed with my daughter.
I had been trying to get in contact with her for days
and it seemed like she was ignoring my calls and texts.
In reality, she was exhausted from working six days a week
and simply hadn't had the energy to call.

What I needed to contact her about was important.
I was feeling more than a little put out because my child
was having issues with keeping in touch with me.

And then I felt Your Spirit whisper, "I understand.
You've been busy this last month, and I've missed our talks.
I've missed you calling out to Me and meeting with Me.
I am concerned about you, My child.
Draw near to Me, and I will draw near to you."

Oh, Abba Father...please forgive me.
I am guilty of doing exactly what my daughter did.
Except I did it to my Creator and King.

I've missed our time together, also.

I've heard the whisper of Your voice in my soul,
calling me, gently drawing me back to You.
I've felt Your Spirit blow through me
like a wind that gently rustles the leaves.
Like a delicate perfume wafting by on the breeze,
inspiring me to breathe deeply before its essence is gone.

But I've been too busy to answer.

Help me to remember to call You, Father.

Especially when I'm busy.

Be Still

Angry. Fuming. Livid. White-hot.
Trembling with anger.

Kneel before the Shepherd,

Be still.
Know that He is God.

He tenderly brushes His hand across my scalp,
down my hair, down my back.
Electric, ethereal clouds, blowing with no breeze,
flow off of and out of my hair.
He does it again. And again. And again.

Peace settles down on me; my anger abates.

He rests His hand on my head.
"Be still and know that I am God."

Deep breath in, then out.

Peace.
Be still.
Truly, He is God.
~~~~~~~~~
Thank You, Lord.
After an argument with my son, I was livid.
All I could do was kneel at Your feet and release it to You.
Thank You for the visual, and for the ensuing peace from Your Spirit.
Thank You for nudging me back to Your path.
You are merciful and gracious, and I long to live for You all of my days.

In Your most holy Name I pray...
Amen.

Be Still, Part 2

In debt.
Exhausted, mentally and physically.
Disobedient. Depressed. Overwhelmed.
Trembling with shame.

Kneel before the Shepherd,

Be still.
Know that He is God.

He tenderly brushes the back of His hand
across my cheek to wipe away the tears,
then pulls me toward His chest,
enfolding me in a gentle embrace.

I can hear His heart beating...
steady, strong, reassuring.

Peace settles down on me
as my tears and shame ebb away.

Speaking softly, He gently kisses the top of my head.
"Be still, My child, and know that I Am God."

A contented sigh.
Then another.

Peace.
Be still.

Truly, He is God.

Focus

Gracious Lord, Mighty Shepherd, Fearsome Protector...
I feel like such a failure.

Bills unpaid or paid late.
Unable to get on/stay on healthier lifestyle.
Can't remember to refill or take my medications.
Broke due to poor financial choices.
House is a mess.
Maintenance neglected.
No energy.

And then I hear the whisper of Your Spirit to mine,
"Don't focus on what, focus on Who!"

Please help me to focus on You, Lord Jesus,
instead of focusing on what's wrong with me and my life.
You created me, and not to be a failure!
Help me to trust You and Your plans for my life.
You know my inner workings far better than I do.
You are in charge of my life and You will provide for my needs.
Help me to understand the difference between my "needs" and my "wants."
You want me to love, honor, and trust You.
That's what I want, too.

Help me to quit focusing on the problems in my life
and start focusing on You instead.
Because instead of telling You how big my problems are,
I should be telling my problems how big my God is!

Gracious Lord, Mighty Shepherd, Fearsome Protector...
thank You for Your gracious love, mercy, and compassion.
Thank You for the quiet whisper of Your Spirit to mine.

I love You.

Questions

Lord, I don't know how to face this trial.

So many questions are coursing through my heart and mind,
but in the end I find myself shushing them as one would quiet a baby.

Because in the end,
I trust You.

I give these questions,
along with the doubts, fears, and unbelief that accompany them,
to You.

I place them in Your hands where they belong,
for You are fully capable of handling anything I am facing.

Regardless of what happens You are...
The Almighty.
The Righteous Lord.
The Master of My Life.
The God Who Sees Me.
...and I love and trust You.

You may scare me at times,
but there is nowhere I would rather be than
squarely in the palm of Your hand.
You are with me
every single step of the way.

Please give me Your peace that passes understanding,
and shelter me in the shadow of Your wings.

In Your precious and holy Name I pray...
Amen.

So Much

So much
to think
about in
the dead
of night.
To worry about and to obsess over. So much for You
to help me work out and understand as only You can.
So much for me to nail to the cross because You are fully
capable of
handling
any of my
problems
and life's
issues. So
much love,
forgiveness,
compassion,
mercy, grace.
So much peace
from You to me.
So much of Your
faithfulness to me, none of
which I deserve, yet You pour
it over me anyway. So much of
You for the rest of my days and
then forevermore. Thank You, my
King and Shepherd. My Lord. I love You.

So much.

Heal This Land

Lord God, I plea for this spiritually blind,
deaf, and stubborn nation of ours.
We have walked away from You,
seeking our own will and rejecting Yours.

The enemy is having a field-day with this country
on so many different levels.
From subtle lies to outrageous manipulation,
he's undermining the structure so that he can move in for the kill.

We have let him.

We have chosen to look the other way
while abhorrent sins have become "the norm".

We have not stood our ground for You
and told the enemy, "Begone!"

We have allowed him to have more and more power until suddenly
he seems to be in the ruling majority regardless of party affiliation.

We deserve and have earned nothing except
Your righteous judgment due to our own hardheartedness.
But I plea that You pour Your mercy, compassion,
and healing over this land.
Because as much as the enemy wants us to believe it's too late,
he is not the one in control.
You are.

Show us our sins and how we can come back to You as a nation.
Soften the collective heart of the land, heal it, and draw us back to You.
Let us again be a nation that honors You as the One True and Living God.
In Your precious, holy, and righteous Name I pray...
Amen.

Pride of a Nation

Precious Savior, I come before You with a heart both heavy and light.
Heavy because I see this nation turning its back on You
and going its own way out of selfish pride and foolish arrogance.
In an era of "whatever floats your boat", many are choosing
to walk away from You and Your plan for their lives.
Worldly desires and wants are higher on their priority list
than any spiritual or eternal needs.

I am loathe to say that I find it acceptable.
I cannot.
I will not.

Just as You allowed the people of Israel to become captive
to other nations because of their refusal to follow You,
I fear the same thing will happen to this nation.
If we do not change our ways it is only a matter of time.

And yet my heart lightens when I remember the long-term outcome.
While this life is temporary, eternity is forever.
If the trials of this life are what it takes to draw us back to you,
as a nation and individually, we have no one to blame but ourselves.
It is to our benefit to endure Your discipline
because You can use for good what the enemy intends for evil.
And even though this nation has forsaken You, You have never forsaken us.
Help us mount an army to fight back, Lord.
An army of warriors on their knees,
praying and seeking Your heart and will.
Equip us, Lord.
Equip me.
Help us turn back to You as a nation once again, Lord,
that we may bless, honor and glorify You in all that we say and do.

In Your righteous, matchless Name I pray...
Amen.

Wherever I Go

You are with me wherever I go and whatever I'm doing.

Sitting at the kitchen table.
Working in my office.
Praising You at church.
Commuting to and from work.
Writing.
Singing in my car.
Sleeping in the dead of night.
Studying Your Word.
Driving to the store.
Going on a mission trip.
Surfing the Internet.
Sitting in the doctor's office.
Posting on social media.
Walking on the beach.
Watching TV.
Praying.
Having a disagreement with someone.

Wherever I am, there You are.
Whatever I'm doing, You are there.

Help me to live my faith out, Lord.
To be Your hands, feet, and voice no matter the cost.
Give me Your wisdom and help me to walk the path as You would.
Help me to walk in faith, knowing that You are with me wherever I go.
Whatever I do.

Send me, Lord. Send me.
Wherever. Whatever.

In Your most holy Name I pray...
Amen.

Action Steps

Lord, help me take steps toward true repentance.
Steps that will draw me closer to You.

Not baby steps, but huge steps.
Strides that rapidly eat up ground.

Help me.
Please.

To hold You in higher esteem than I hold myself.
To wholeheartedly love and trust You.
To take a step of faith and know that you will catch me.
To rest in You and know that You are "enough".
To live the way You intended when You formed me.
To pursue Your higher calling no matter the cost.

Help me, Lord Jesus.

Please forgive me for my selfish behavior
and teach me the beauty of Your ways.

Give me Your strength, will, and wisdom to live for You.
Now and forevermore.

In Your glorious Name I pray...
Amen.

Adrift

Lord Jesus, I felt so confused and adrift
after my granddaughter passed away.

I wrote the "I See You" poem for my daughter,
yet You gave it to me as a gift from Your heart to mine.

You met me exactly where I was with exactly what I needed.
Though my eyes were blind with grief,
Yours weren't.

Thank You.

My heart and soul still tremble when I remember...
How strong Your Presence was that evening,
as I heard You whisper those words to my soul.
How completely undone I was by Your grace, mercy, and compassion.
How You opened my eyes at just the right moment
to understand the length, depth, and width
of Your love and compassion.

I am still undone.

Thank You for loving me enough to reach down
and touch my grieving heart with Yours.

Help me, my Lord.
To see Your hand and heart in every part of my life.
To see what changes I need to make.
To draw ever closer to You and Your loving heart.

In Your precious and matchless Name I pray...
Amen.

Death

Father God,
You did not create us to have to experience or deal with death.
It's contrary to everything You wanted for us.
Due to human nature we made that choice of our own free will,
but it wasn't something You intended for us to experience.
A single choice created a cascade effect,
one that has affected all humans since Adam and Eve.
They chose to walk away from Your will...
with devastating consequences.

And yet...
while You disciplined them, You did not forsake them.
From before the beginning of time
You knew that they would disobey You,
so You promised to send a Redeemer;
One with power over life and death.

And You did.
Those who trust in Him will live with You for all of eternity.
But until then we must deal with the cascade effect
from Adam and Eve's choice.

The pain of losing loved ones is all too real.

I seek Your comforting arms in this time of grief.
Pour Your balm of peace down on those of us grieving right now
and help us to feel You near.
Give us moments of respite when we need them.
Help us know what to do to ease each others pain
and how to comfort one another.
Please draw us close to You, Lord,
and let us feel the comfort of Your embrace.
In Your precious, priceless, eternal Name I pray...
Amen.

Bending Near

Just as I sat down to spend time with You this morning,
my granddaughter woke up and came out of her bedroom,
cheerfully chattering away at me on a number of subjects.
I wasn't frustrated, but I found I kept losing my concentration.

It made me stop and wonder how
You perceive me when I'm chattering away to You,
sharing my thoughts, prayers, and interests.

Do You just nod Your head and say, "Uh-huh..."
and keep doing what You're doing,
not really listening to me?

Or do You stop, bend near,
and take time with me?

My heart and soul already know the answer.

Father God, please help me to be more like You.
Help me to learn the skill of stopping, bending near,
and taking time with my loved ones and others.

Please continue to mold me in Your image, Lord,
until Your return.

In Your precious and exquisite Name I pray...
Amen.

Part Three: Allegory

"Like ripples in a pond,
Your Spirit is stirring my soul..."
~ *"Ripples"*

Renovation

In a series of moments
that brought me to my knees before You,
You introduced me to the Translator...
Your Holy Spirit.
And You didn't just introduce me...
You allowed Him to reside inside of me
in order to help me understand You,
grow in You, and be touched by Your heart.

Before that moment,
Your Truth was a confusing jumble
of thoughts and words that rambled on,
making no sense to my all-too-human nature.

I could not understand
because I did not speak the language of Love
and I did not know the One Who could translate it for me.

Though I thought I knew and loved You,
it was a superficial, selfish, uneasy knowledge and love.

But the Spirit changed all of that in an instant.

When He first set up residence,
He leveled the antiquated shack
I had laboriously and painfully cobbled together over the years.
It was rickety, leaning, and dangerous to one and all.
He removed the ramshackle disaster in the blink of an eye
and began to clear the ground for a sturdier, stronger, eternal foundation.
One upon which He could build,
expanding and remodeling as necessary.

He has been faithfully building ever since.

Lord, I cannot help but be dumbstruck at times
over the magnitude, intricacy, and beauty of His structure.

Over the years He has taught me Your language of Love,
speaking it to me throughout the day, in the darkness of night,
and even whispering it to me in my dreams.

He took a simple, unlovely, lonely child and helped me understand
that You see me as a beloved, beautiful, treasured daughter.
One that You valued more than life itself.
One that You long to talk to
so that I can know You as You know me.

Thank You, my Lord.
For never giving up on me, though I had given up on myself.
For loving me faithfully despite my tawdry unfaithfulness.
For the indwelling of Your Holy Spirit,
Who opened My eyes, ears, heart and soul to Your Truth
and Who whispers Your love and guidance to my heart and soul.

Please help me to be Your hands, feet, and voice
that others may realize that You see them
as beloved, beautiful, and treasured.
When they look at me,
let them see
You.

Help them to understand
that You value them more than life itself,
and that You long to be in relationship with them
so that they can know You
as You know them.

Introduce them to the Translator, my Lord,
that they may begin to understand.

Living Water

Water.

When I'm truly thirsty,
I love the feelings I get as I drink it.
It satisfies.
It quenches.
It's so refreshing it's almost heady.

I can instantly feel changes in my body,
down to a microscopic level,
almost as if my body is sighing in relief.
Knowing it was dehydrated.
Knowing its reserves were dangerously low.

But all of those feelings, my Lord, pale in comparison
to You, Your Spirit, and Your Living Water.

While there may be similar analogies,
that is where the likeness ends.
You satisfy and quench my spiritual thirst.
Not just for the moment, but forever.
A mere moment in Your Presence was so heady
that it changed my life for all eternity.
I have longed, since that day,
for the moment I will be in Your Presence forever.

The changes that were wrought in my spirit that night,
and since, have altered my spiritual DNA on a subatomic level.
For that I will always be grateful.

Because while I may not know the specifics, as You do,
I know my spiritual reserves were dangerously low.
My soul was gasping, crying out, dying from thirst
when You came near, stooped down,

and eternally refilled it with Living Water.
Do I love the Living Water You provide?
Yes. Enthusiastically, emphatically *yes!*

But "love" isn't even a word that truly applies.
Not because it's untrue, but because it's so inadequate in its scope.
It doesn't even begin to encompass the magnitude of how it makes me feel.

Love?
Yes.

But also...
Grateful. Unworthy. Redeemed. Treasured.
Flabbergasted. Awed. Accepted. Chosen.
Indebted. Freed. Encouraged. Rescued. Known. Completed.
Loved. Adopted.
By One Whose love cannot, and will not, ever fail me.

There is nothing that I can do that will ever make You stop loving me.
And that is the headiest feeling of all.

Thank You, Lord.

While my love pales pathetically in comparison to Yours,
I cannot help but tell You that
I am falling, tumbling, careening...
head-over-heels in love with You.

You take my breath away
in ways I cannot even begin to describe.
You are my Faithful Shepherd.
Love Incarnate.
My Beloved.
And I live to serve You.

All the days of my life.

Intertwined

Lord, there is no part of my life story where You are not intertwined.
Nowhere that Your gold thread cannot be seen weaving
throughout the tapestry of my life.

Protecting me.
Reaching out to me.
Comforting me.
Rescuing me.
Forgiving me.
Welcoming me back.
Saving me.
Admonishing me.
Loving me unconditionally.

Your thread shines brightly amidst the darkness of life.

I did nothing to deserve Your...
Love.
Grace.
Salvation.
Forgiveness.
Compassion.
Protection.
Influence.
Mercy.
...yet You freely extend them to me anyway.

You graciously, lovingly, patiently drew me in
until I fell head~over~heels in love with You.

I am humbled, amazed, and dumbstruck at times
that You would bother with such an imperfect vessel.

And yet...

isn't that where Your glory shines the brightest?
In imperfect vessels unable to attain the necessary changes on their own?
Who are solely and completely dependent upon You
for the remodeling and renovation You have in mind?
Who cannot "get there from here"?
Who are willing to acknowledge that the Architect behind the design
must be the One to save them?

With that in mind, it all makes sense.

Because I am a hot mess who will never
"get there from here" under my own power.

Without You, I'm done.
Kaput. Finished. Condemned.

But with You,
I see hope rising exponentially.
I see Grace. Life. Eternity.

I am a work-in-progress
who is being shaped, formed, and sculpted into Your image.
I do it so very imperfectly at times, but with Your help
I keep trying.
Keep persevering.
Keep trusting.

For You are my story.
You are the glorious gold thread that shines in my tapestry.

When I let You mold and shape me,
I become one of the countless threads You are using
to create a brilliant, vibrant, eternal tapestry
that tells the story of the Living God
and how much He loves His children.

And there is no place I would rather be.

Lifeline

My Lord,
how often my thoughts now turn to you throughout the day.
What a joy and delight it is to my soul,
for such has not always been the case.

After years of feeling as if I had fallen overboard into frigid waters,
Your Spirit gently broke through my resistance
and helped me to realize that I hadn't fallen overboard.
I had chosen to dive off.

Away from the safety of Your vessel.

Well over my head in dangerous waters,
I thrashed and struggled,
all without realizing my Rescuer was only a breath away.

I was drowning,
yet in my stubborn ignorance I never reached for Your hand.

So
gently,
persistently,
You whispered my
name and reached out to me.
You calmed my thrashing soul
and then You threw me a Lifeline.
You
rescued me.
And my life will never be the same.

Diamonds

Carbon. Rocks. Heat. Pressure.

Misunderstood. Ignored. Passed by. Ugly.

Found. Known. Valued. Rescued.

Uncovered. Developed. Faceted. Polished.

Esteemed. Appreciated. Desired. Beautiful.

Treasured. Loved. Priceless.

Redeemed.

Deeply Rooted

I can hear the wind
blowing through the trees outside my window.
At times the leaves barely move
as the gentle breeze softly caresses them.

At other times gusts of wind,
unseen without the witness of the tree,
whip and shake the tree to its very core.

Bending to the will of the wind,
moving, flexing, and jostling
as it is blown hither and yon,
the tree will likely survive.
Leaves may be lost in the process but later,
in another season of its life,
evidence of growth and maturity
will be made manifest.

But for now,
in order to survive the wind,
it must bend and sway the way its Creator intended.
Because a decision to stand firm,
staunchly resistant to the wind
and unwilling to be flexible to its surroundings,
would truly be its downfall.
The storms of life would be its death knell
because it cannot withstand the Power it struggles against.

Help me, O Lord,
to bend and sway in the storms of life
knowing that You, my Creator, are right beside me.
For while You may allow the storms to blow,
as long as I am deeply rooted in You
I can withstand hurricanes.

The Rarest Bloom

One day a vase found itself in the trash heap.

Broken beyond repair, discarded, considered worthless by most,
it knew it was only a matter of time before it would be destroyed.
While it had once been useful, and a thing of beauty,
now it was chipped, cracked, and leaky.
No glory or beauty could ever again come from the vase itself.

And the vase knew it.

But the Rarest of Blooms saw the vase and Its Heart was moved.
The Bloom saw beyond the ugliness of the vase's chips and cracks.
It saw not what it was, or what it had been, but what it could become.

The Bloom said,
"I want *that* vase.
That vase will know its beauty can only come from Me."

When the Rarest Bloom was placed in the sad little vase,
the container was completely transformed.
It was made more beautiful and radiant than when it had been new.
And while it did not always serve the Rarest Bloom perfectly,
it served the Bloom joyfully.
For it knew that its glory and beauty came not from itself
but from the Bloom within.

Thank You, Lord Jesus.
For transforming this exceedingly cracked, imperfect vessel
into a container to hold Your priceless Spirit.
For allowing Your Light to shine bright and strong in spite of my humanity,
letting It burst through my wounds that they might be healed,
while allowing others to realize the extent of Your Beauty.

For being the Rarest Bloom in all of eternity.

Ripples

Moving. Stirring. Transforming.

Like
ripples in a
pond, Your Spirit
is stirring in my soul,
creating ever-widening
rings that bounce and
reverberate in all
areas of my
life.
Your Spirit
is causing a cascade
effect, the beauty of each
ripple is being made ever more
manifest as it touches others and creates
an infinite number of ripples echoing through
each life it touches. As the Spirit touches and
moves one person, so that person then touches
another, who touches another, who touches
another. Each transformation creates
infinitely widening ripples of
a gracious, loving Spirit
Who etches
Himself
on
our
s
o
u
l
s
.

Uprooting

A plant lies on the ground.

Dug up.
Roots exposed.
Vulnerable.

No moisture or nutrition is coming in.
It is reliant only upon its own meager resources.

The heat of the sun beats down on it.

A clump of dirt
clings tenaciously.
Soon even it will dry up and fall away,
truly leaving the plant on its own.

Unless and until it is transplanted to good soil, and nurtured,
it will continue to fail until it is too late.

Eventually the plant itself will whither and die,
never understanding
how dangerous its situation had been,
or that the process began as soon as it was uprooted.
It just doesn't know that yet.

If you aren't rooted in Christ,
you have more in common
with that plant
than you realize.

Don't wait until it's too late.

Seek Him while He may be found. [22.]

Master Gardener

I was a rebellious rosebush; He is the Master Gardener.
I was growing wild...unsightly, ungainly, and out-of-control.
He rescued me and brought me to His workbench.
I fought against Him at first,
but my thorns were no match for His tender touch.
Because even though some of my thorns pricked Him and made Him bleed,
He was never anything other than gentle with me.
He loved me in spite of my thorns.
Maybe even because of them.

Over time, I've found myself falling in love with this Master Gardener.
I've found that I cannot live without His tender touch,
and that I cannot thrive without His faithful steadfastness.
I see Him smiling and hear Him softly humming
as He tenderly prunes and trims me as He sees fit.
Removing broken branches and dead leaves,
enriching the soil surrounding me to encourage growth,
He never removes or adds more than necessary...
it's always just the right amount.
He whispers words of encouragement to me.
He lets me know that He believes in me.
That I will flourish under His tender loving care.
That my roots will grow deep during times of trial,
and that they should always source themselves in Him
during times of drought and hardship.
That my growth is for His glory, not my own.
That I can trust in Him and His plans for my life.
That the beauty of my blossoms will benefit others
and that they will release a delightful aroma like no other.
His voice comforts me, and I know that I am safe in His hands.
For though I was a rebellious rosebush, He loves me in spite of myself.
And I love Him.

For He is my beloved Master Gardener.

Master Gardener, Revisited

I offer up my life and my will as a sacrifice to You,
as well as the unkempt garden of my heart and soul,
to do with what You will.

I yearn to honor You in all that I do, my Lord,
not dishonor You.

Help me in my unbelief,
for You are my Master Gardener.

While my spirit is willing,
my flesh is feeble and traitorous.
Till the soil, remove the noxious weeds,
and plant the fruits of Your Spirit.
Let them bloom and flourish,
bearing a bumper crop year after year,
until I am Home with You.

I choose to release control to You, Lord,
in order to bear fruit that pleases You.
For when I am in charge,
weeds proliferate and chaos reigns.

Help me to faithfully honor and serve You in all areas of my life.
Every breath.
Every blossom.
Every fruit.
Every harvest.
Until You call me Home.

And then
forevermore.

Sweet Aroma

Feeling called.
Pulled.
Enticed.
Yet not against my will.

Like a delightful aroma tantalizing my senses,
knowing it promises good things to come,
I find I cannot help myself...
I am drawn to get up and go find the Source.

Like bacon or coffee first thing in the morning;
like an exotic bloom whose delicate smell permeates the area;
like a sumptuous feast cooked by the finest chef...
the Scent draws me in, compelling me to follow.

Yet even those comparisons are heavy-handed.
Crude. Inadequate.

It is the scent of a beloved Shepherd to his lost and weary sheep.
Bleating, they come running.
Knowing He will protect and care for them.
Knowing He has their best interest at heart.
Knowing that, regardless of any obstacles they encounter,
they can trust His faithful love for them.

Thank You, Lord Jesus.
For loving me.
Calling me.
Caring for me.
Protecting me.

Thank You for being the Sweet Aroma in my life,
gently enticing me to seek You out,
that I may live.

One Drop

One drop. Just one.

I was stained. Putrid.
Dying from the inside out.

One drop was all it took.

Washing. Flooding. Purifying.
Stain-free. Cleansed. Alive like never before.
The masterpiece is not yet finished.
The paint is still wet.
One day the Master will complete the collection
He began so many years ago.

But one drop was all that was needed.

Thank You, Lord Jesus.
For drawing near that I might be saved.
For Your faithfulness despite the depth of my humanity.
For the joy and peace deep in my soul.
For Your sacrifice being "enough".
For that very first drop of blood, and all that came afterward.
For deciding I was worth the trouble.
For being my Master and allowing me to be Your bond-servant.

You, O King, are my Everything.
I lift up my hands, heart, soul, voice, and all that I am to You.
They are a meager offering, Lord, but all that I am and have
are Yours to do with as You will.
Help me to be faithful, my Shepherd.
Give me Your strength and wisdom that I may follow Your lead.

In Your beloved Name I pray...
Amen.

Contentment

Contentment is spreading throughout my life, Lord,
accompanied by Your peace and joy.
A contentment that comes in spite of the trials that I face,
it is a deep, living well-spring that quenches my soul's thirst.
An abiding peace that does not, and cannot,
come from within myself; it can only come from You.

As my steps fall in line with Yours,
as my rebellious spirit comes under Your calming hand,
as my fears are placed on the altar of my soul as a sacrifice for You,
I find the well-spring growing.

First it was a trickle seeping up through stony ground.
Then a rivulet where I could rest and refresh myself when I was weary.
And now it is becoming an oasis
where I can stop and tarry for awhile as I meet with You,
enjoying the beauty nurtured by Your presence.
It is an oasis spreading as far as the eye can see.
Lush, vibrant, and restorative to my soul.

Thank You, beloved Lord, for this deep peace
and contentment that I neither created nor expected.

Thank You for being such a gracious, mighty, and generous
Savior, Lord, and Master.

You give me so much more than I have ever deserved,
and I praise and thank You for Your abundance.
Love. Mercy. Forgiveness. Salvation.
Joy. Contentment. Peace that passes understanding.

For all of this and so much more...thank You.

I love You.

When Love Passed By

Weak and mortally wounded by my sins,
I was laying by the side of the road with no hope that anyone could help.

And then You came along.

I had met You before, but only from a distance.
This was up-close and personal.
It was the difference between night and day.
Shadows and sunlight. Death and life.

With tender, loving care, You performed a miracle.
You brought back to life a soul that was barely breathing,
that had been teetering on the edge of death's door.
In one fell swoop You burst through the door,
paid my ransom, and rescued me from the enemy.
You helped lift my head when I was too weak to do so myself.

Even if only a glimpse, You showed me Who You are...
and in the process changed my life for all eternity.

Thank You, Lord Jesus.
Mere words cannot convey my gratitude.
Your Spirit must translate the groanings
of my own soul's feeble attempts,
for I am wholly inadequate to the task.
But I will gladly spend the rest of my life, whatever time I have left,
telling others of Your gracious, glorious love
and Your magnificent and compassionate ways.
For while You are indescribable,
so much can be told of You and Your mighty ways.
Help me to tell of when Love passed by...
and what a difference it made in my life.

For all eternity.

Part Four: Meditation

"Sitting quietly in Your presence.
Hearing the sound of my own breathing.
Slowing down my thoughts.
Slowing down my breathing..."
~ *"Heartbeat"*

Drawing Near

Though I'm mentally and physically exhausted...
Though my schedule was hectic yesterday
and will be no different today...
Though my body is achy and in pain...

I want to slow down my heart, soul, and life
and spend time with You, My Lord.

Not my phone, computer, or any other distraction.
Not even my family.

Just You.

My soul aches with longing for the day I will see You face-to-face.

My spirit soars and is completely undone
at the merest glimpse of Your Presence.

You are the mightiest of all,
glorious beyond comprehension.

You are the Beginning of all
and You will be the End of all.

Your fingerprint is on every molecule
that makes up this universe.

Though I have been a rebellious wretch,
spiritually deaf and blind to Your Majesty,
still You call out to me.

Seeking to open my eyes and ears.
Seeking relationship with me.
Seeking to save me from the enemy.

Your love and Presence roll over me like a flash flood,
overwhelming my senses,
bringing me to my knees.

Tears flow unchecked as I meet with my God.
King.
Savior.
Creator.
Friend.

Your love knows no bounds.

I simply could not dream up a god as good as You are.

Your faithfulness is immeasurable.
No one will ever plumb the depths of Your mercy.
Your grace is a priceless treasure.
Your forgiveness and love are without equal.

Thank You, Lord God,
for this opportunity to draw near to You.
To worship and glorify You.
To call You my Redeemer.
To sit at Your feet.

Thank You, beloved Shepherd.
For loving me enough to not let me stay where I was,
mired deep in the enemy's clutches.
For setting me free.
For giving me new Life.
For letting me be Your hands, feet, and voice
that others may also draw near.
For calling me Your own.

In Your matchless, glorious, and holy Name I pray...
Amen.

Releasing Control

I'm just quietly sitting here, Lord.

Waiting on You.
Soaking in Your Presence.
Relearning once again that there's nothing I can do
to make myself more, or less, acceptable to You.

You love me just as I am.

You're not waiting for me to attain perfection before seeking You.
You simply want me to draw near.
Not in spite of all my fears and failures,
but because of them.
Because of my absolute dependence on Your grace,
mercy, forgiveness, compassion, and strength.

It's the relationship You want,
not the checking-off of impossible goals.

You want my...
Heart.
Soul.
Love.
Life.
Talents and faults.
Loyalty and unbelief.
Trust and fears.

You want everything.
All of me,
for good or for bad,
willingly given back to You.
A gift from the created to the Creator.
A gift of sacrificial proportion

given without trying to maintain control.
Done in faith. Trust. Love.

Lord Jesus, once again I release control to You.
I irrevocably release all that I have,
all that I am,
and all that I will ever be to You,
my precious and beloved Master,
to use as You will.

Lead me, Father,
for I can be a stubborn, foolish child...
yet one that longs to do Your will.

Guide my path so that it follows Yours.
Pour Your Holy Spirit down, and let my life
be a pleasing sacrifice to You, Your glory, and Your honor.

Send angelic warriors to intercede on my behalf, as needed,
to keep the enemy and his minions at bay.

Use me, Lord.
Let me be Your hands, feet, and voice in all that I do,
but let me do nothing to detract from You and Your glory.

I ask only for Your strength, faith, and wisdom as we journey together.

In Your most holy Name I pray...
Amen.

Waking Up

Waking up.

Coming into Your presence
with a joyful, grateful heart.

Sitting next to You,
leaning on Your shoulder.

Feeling the welcoming embrace.

Hearing Your slow, steady,
and reassuring heartbeat.

Feeling the warmth,
both physical and spiritual,
radiating from You.

Knowing that I am safe. Wanted. Loved.
In spite of myself.

Thank You, Lord Jesus.

To You be all glory,
honor,
and praise.

None deserve it
more than You.

Your Eyes

Help me to focus on You, Lord.

Help me to lift my eyes
above the confines of this sin-stained world
and let me gaze into Your eyes, heart, and soul.

For it is there that I truly find myself, Lord.

Who You intended me to be.
Who I long to be.

Everything else in this world dims and fades
into the background when I gaze into Your eyes
and allow You to gaze into mine.

Everything falls into place.

The peace in my soul tells me
that I am precisely where I need to be
and a contented sigh
passes my lips.

Eternity

At times it seems our lives here on earth last an eternity.
And yet it's only a drop in the bucket.
Not even a drop.

Because true eternity begins with You, Lord.

Looking back over our lives,
we think of eternity as a subjective time-frame.

It's not something we enjoy.
We endure it. We tolerate it.

Waiting in line seems to last an eternity.

A contraction during labor feels like an eternity.

Waiting for Your return seems nothing short of an eternity.

And yet in the end it's all an illusion contrary to reality.
The longest life here on earth is nothing but a blip in comparison.

This moment, this blip when we are here on earth,
isn't even equivalent to time spent
in the waiting room of a doctor's office.

In eternal time it's far shorter than a nanosecond.

When we depart this life, we will truly begin eternity.
With You or without You.

It's our choice.

But we need to choose now.
Or the choice will be made for us.

The Gift of a Void

My spirit is tired.

I realize it's been days since I've spent quality time with You,
sitting down at Your feet and listening for Your voice.

Quiet.
Waiting.
Attentive.

I've spent moments with You,
sandwiched in between errands and commitments,
but it's not the same.

When I don't intentionally begin my day with You,
blocking out the world so I can meet with my Creator,
I feel a gaping void.

My soul knows something is missing.
Something important.

Yet even the void itself is a gift and a treasure,
for without it I wouldn't feel the need to seek You.

And You...
You are Everything to me.

Help me to remember that, Lord.

Help me to be intentional about meeting with You.

Help me to be intentional
about sitting at the feet of,
and listening attentively to the gentle voice of,
my beloved Master.

Heartbeat

Sitting quietly in Your presence.

Hearing the sound of my own breathing

Slowing down my thoughts.

Slowing down my breathing.

Relaxing.

Focusing on You.

Listening for Your still, small voice.

Listening for Your heartbeat.

Feeling Your Spirit stir within my soul.

Peace. Joy. Rest.

All in,

and because of,

You.

Quiet Time

I love waking up before my alarm goes off
and realizing I get to spend time with You.

Whispering "Good morning, Lord", I can't help but smile.
The white noise of the world fades into the background
as I feel Your Spirit and Your Peace wash over me.

You and Your Spirit are with me
whether I can "feel" You or not, and You always will be.
But I'm grateful for the confirmation I feel from Your Spirit to mine.
When I slow down my heart, mind, and soul to focus on You.
When I empty myself of worries, fears, and distractions,
laying them all at Your feet along with my will.
When I make a conscious choice to die to self
for Your glory and honor.
When I feel Your gentle arms envelop me.
To comfort me. To rescue me. To shelter me. To shepherd me.
To affirm, once again, Your love for me
as well as Your grace, mercy, and forgiveness.

Thank You, Lord Jesus.

Help me to focus on You throughout the day,
and help me to continue dying to self on a daily basis.
Give me Your peace that passes understanding,

All for,
and because of,
Your glory.

In Your priceless, magnificent Name I pray...
Amen.

Part Five: Thanksgiving

"Thank You, beloved Savior.
For being here in the good times and the bad..."
~ *"Thank You"*

In Good Company

Lord Jesus,
I feel such a kindred connection
with both Peter and Mary Magdalene.

They aren't my "role models",
as that space is reserved for You,
but I feel like I'm in good company with them.
They both monumentally screwed up, yet You forgave them
and counted them among Your closest friends.

I pray that is the case with me, Lord.

That even though I screw up far too often,
for I am a weak and double-minded child,
You know that I love You more than words can express.
I pray that You have a soft spot in Your heart
for this wayward soul.

Because even though I'm a mess, You say that I'm *Your* mess,
bought and paid for with Your own precious blood,
and I'm eternally grateful for all You have done for me.

You are my beloved Master.
My Shepherd.
My Life.
My Breath.
My Everything.

You are the Reason I get up in the morning
and the Pillow I lay my head down on at night.

You are Faithful and True, even when I am not,
and You gently draw me back into the fold when I wander away.

Your mercy is boundless, Your love is bottomless,
and Your grace is unfailing.

You meet me where I am at,
no matter how grim the circumstances,
and You comfort me with Your tender Spirit.

I could easily fall into the pools
of love and compassion I see in Your eyes.

As much of a mess as I am,
as well as You know me,
You still love me.

For that I will never cease to be grateful.

Thank You, my beloved Lord and Master,
for all You have done, are doing, and ever will do
to turn this chipped, broken vessel
into Your vision of what I can be through Your Spirit.

It will only and ever be
by Your strength and compassion
that such a change is possible.
That I could *ever* "get there from here."

So if I am similar to Peter and Mary Magdalene, Lord,
I thank and praise You for such similarities.
All the credit, all the glory, can only and ever be Yours.

I wouldn't want it any other way.

No More Shackles

Thank You, Father God.
For allowing Your Son to be my righteousness.
For letting me replace my filthy rags with His spotless robes.
For making my sins as white as snow.

Were it not for Him and His sacrifice(s),
I would never be worthy of Your love, grace, mercy, and forgiveness.

Thank You for freeing me of the bondage of sin, guilt, and shame.

I was shackled by the enemy,
bound tightly in chains I couldn't see.

I never really knew or understood
the depth of my imprisonment
until You released me
and I tasted the sweet nectar of Your freedom.

True freedom.
Eternal freedom.

Now I am Yours,
and You are mine.
Forevermore.

Thank You.

The Tenth Leper

Precious Lord, how much of my life have I spent
either not being close to You or taking You for granted?
Even now, despite my desire to serve You,
I'm guilty of that behavior at times.

You are amazingly generous and compassionate,
yet how many times am I like one of the ten lepers that You healed? [23.]
Nine of them ran off without thanking You.
Only one stopped, turned around,
and went back to thank You.

Please forgive me, Lord,
for spending so much of my life as "one of the nine".

I choose to be the tenth leper.

I choose to stop, turn around, and fall flat on my face
to praise, worship, and thank You.
For stepping down and sacrificing Yourself that I might live.
For being my Savior.
For healing my spirit.
For walking with me day-by-day.
For loving me in spite of myself.
For being my First Love.
For loving me first.

For everything.

You are magnificent, Lord,
mighty in all of Your ways,
and I choose to thank and worship You
all the days of my life.

Grace

Grace.
Such a small word.
One syllable. Two vowels. Three consonants.
Barely a breath of a word.

But oh, such a word!

A word that encompasses eternity.
A word larger than the universe.
A word that showers down incomprehensible love and compassion.
A word that lifts up the head of the weary,
heartsick travelers of this world and gives them hope.
A word that shines like a beacon, cutting through the inky darkness
that surrounds our souls and rescues the lost from tempestuous seas.
A word that paid a debt it didn't owe
in order to rescue those who had a debt they could never pay.
Not because it had to do so, but because it chose to do so.
Wanted to do so.
Ached to do so.

Such a small word, yet as large as eternity itself.

Thank You, Lord Jesus, for grace.
For inviting and allowing me through the Door to Your Kingdom
even though I'm not worthy to knock on that Door.
For being willing to look past who I was without You
to whom I could become with You.

Thank You, Beautiful One,
for Your Amazing Grace.

Beauty

Thank You, Lord, for the beauty You have created.

The morning mist on the lake.
The sunrise.
The blue sky with lacy, ephemeral clouds.
They all combine to create a beautiful moment in time.
A reminder of the Divine Creator behind it all.

Thank You, Father God.
For the beauty that surrounds me.
For the thought and care that went into each element of nature.
For being such a considerate Creator.

Beauty,
whether in nature, art, or a child's laugh,
is not necessary for life.

But it completes it in a way
that only a loving God would realize.

Thank You, Father, for beauty.
Open my eyes, that I may see Your Handiwork
surrounding me each moment of every day.

In Your gracious Name I pray...
Amen.

You Are the One

I've missed this, Lord.

I've missed this closeness in relationship between You and me.
This quiet time. Fellowship. Koinonia.

It seems that things simply 'come up'
and get in the way of our time together...
which pleases the enemy to no end.

He's far more *displeased* when,
realizing just how far I've strayed from You,
I scurry back when I hear You call me.

I'm okay with the enemy being displeased,
for You are the One Whose approval I seek.
You are the One Whom I love.
The One for Whom I yearn.
The One Who takes my breath away.

Thank You, Lord Jesus.

For calling, drawing, loving, and forgiving me.
For healing, comforting, teaching, and discipling me.
For Your grace, mercy, forgiveness, and compassion.
For Your sacrifices, faithfulness, persistence, and vigilance.
For everything.

Thank You, Lord.
Master.
Brother.
Friend.

I love You.

Peter

Lord, I can relate to Peter so well.

Brash.
Impetuous.
Hot-headed.
Letting my mouth get ahead of my brain.
Prone to falling flat on my face due to my own impetuous choices.

And yet,
on the other side of that same token...

Loving You more than life itself.
Wanting to stand for You no matter the cost.
Aching to hear You say to me,
"Well done, good and faithful servant."

Lord, Peter was so very human.
It makes me love him all the more for it.
He screwed up on a regular basis,
yet You loved, chose, and accepted him anyway.
And that gives me hope.
Because while I can be a hot mess at times,
I'm *Your* hot mess.

Thank You for making me like Peter, Lord.
Because in the end any change, growth, or improvement
can only be credited to You and Your influence in my life.

I wouldn't want it any other way.

Where My Comfort Lies

In Your infinite wisdom, Lord,
You used my six-month-old granddaughter, Gabriella,
to teach me a lesson in sourcing myself in You.
And what a lesson it was.

She cried inconsolably when my daughter had to leave for awhile.
Suddenly she wailed, "Ma-ma!"
It was painfully obvious she desperately wanted her mother
and that she was truly heart-broken at their separation.
Gabriella finds her rest in, and is comforted by, her mother.
Without her presence and influence, she will eventually fall apart.
Maybe not immediately upon noticing the separation,
but there always comes a time when she simply cannot cope without her.

Oh Lord Jesus, what an example this is of my need for You!
You are where I find my true rest and comfort.
Apart from You and Your guidance, my life begins to unravel.
Maybe not immediately upon noticing the separation,
but there will *always* come a time when I will fall apart
and come running back to Your arms, sobbing, and crying, "Abba!"
Because I am incomplete without You.
It's not a matter of *if* I will fall apart, but *when*.

Like my granddaughter's deep hunger and need for her mother,
You created within me with a deep hunger and need for You.
And Lord, I desperately need You!
Every moment of every day; every nanosecond.
You are my guidance, my defense,
my influence and my righteousness.
And it is only in You that I am truly free!

Thank You, precious Abba, for allowing me to draw near,
and for allowing me to be Your child.
I love You.

Father

Lord God, so many people think they know Who You are.
They are positive that You are judgmental, angry,
uncaring, distant, manipulative, or domineering,
yet they have no clue whatsoever Who You really are.

Their judgment is biased due to earthly influences that blind them,
yet there is no comparison.
The differences are so grand that it's like comparing apples and elephants.
Even the very best earthly father cannot compare to You,
for he can neither escape his humanity nor attain Your deity.

You know, in ways that even I do not,
that my own earthly father had his faults.
While I never consciously compared You with him,
there have still been times the nuances of our relationship
created an unwelcome distance between You and me.
And yet today that distance is gone, as it it never existed,
supplanted by an eternal Love I could never have imagined.

I don't deserve You, Lord. I truly don't.
You freely gave Your life so that I could be adopted into Your family.
So that I could take Your Name as my own.
So that I could call You my Father.
While I don't *truly* know You, I have an inkling.
I've seen glimpses of Your reflection from the corner of my eye.
I've heard Your whisper of love at all hours of the day and night.
The whisper that tells me that I am Yours and You are mine.
That even though I'm a work-in-progress, You feel I'm worth the bother.

Thank You for pursuing me faithfully, even when I was faithless.
For being that voice in the middle of the night.
For Your compassionate healing in my life.
For being the Father I've always wanted and needed.
And for so much more.

Treasured

I'm sitting here,
decidedly less than half-awake.

Tired. Sore.
Definitely 'past my prime'.

Full of faults, foibles, quirks,
and double-mindedness.

And yet I am...

Loved...by Love Incarnate.
Treasured...by the Priceless Jewel.
Adopted...by my Heavenly Father.
Redeemed...by the King of kings.
Rescued...by the Avenging Shepherd.
Forgiven...by the Sinless One.
Pardoned...by the Righteous Judge.
Accepted...by the Man of Sorrows.
Ransomed...by my Beloved.
Faith-filled...by He Who is Faithful.
Transformed...by the Ancient of Days.

Thank You, Lord.

You are amazing.

Mercies

Lord God,
You are gracious and merciful
beyond my comprehension.

Though I am a sinner,
worthy of none of Your grace and mercy,
You have extended them to me without reservation
and adopted me as Your own child.

Though I stumble and fall,
failing over and over again,
still You love me
and do not reject me.

Thank You.

I love You more than mere words can convey.
I am grateful for Your mercies,
new every morning

Help me to be Your bond-servant, my Lord,
this day and all others.

In Your blessed Name I pray...
Amen.

The Little Things

It's the little things, Lord.

It's waking up smiling, before my eyes are even open,
and whispering, 'Good morning, Lord.'
It's feeling You smile in return.

It's biting my tongue, figuratively or literally,
rather than say something that would vex Your Spirit.
It's caring about vexing Your Spirit.

It's catching glimpses of how You see other people,
for good or bad, even if only from the corner of my eye.
It's wanting to see more.

It's apologizing first, even when I wasn't wrong,
in order to be Your witness.
It's meaning it.

It's my heart being filled to overflowing with Your love
and letting it spill over in joy.
It's yearning to share it with others.

It's trying to live my life in such a way that one day
I will hear You tell me, "Well done, good and faithful servant."
It's aching to hear those words.

It's seeing the evidence of Your Spirit in my life,
knowing I could never have done any of it without You.
It's giving You the credit.

It's the little things in my life that are adding up
to the huge things that You are doing in my life, Lord.

It's the little things.

Before My Alarm

Waking up an hour before my alarm,
I realize I have extra time to spend with You, my Lord.
I don't have to do so.
I want to.
I long to.

I find a smile on my face and my soul
at the thought.

Studying.
Singing.
Praying.
Worshiping.
All come down to the same thing:
time spent at the feet of my beloved Lord and Master.

Time spent walking and talking.
Learning and growing.
Drawing battle plans.
Listening
for Your
still, small voice.

Thank You for waking me before my alarm, Lord.

I love You.

Weary Soul

My spirit is weary.

Distractions abounded this morning and I missed our time together.
It set the tone for the day and my heart and soul ached.

I felt the void.

The antithesis of closeness,
it felt wrong on so many levels.

I find myself scurrying back to You and clinging to Your side,
under the protection of Your arm,
where I belong.

Thank You, Lord.

For loving me and desiring a relationship with me.
For giving me the strength to walk the path You have set before me.
For Your Spirit drawing me back to You when I wander.
For the aching void reminding me of my First Love.
For welcoming this prodigal child back to the safety of Your arms.
Again.

For everything.

I love You.

Understanding King David

Thank You, Lord, for drawing me back to Your bottomless well.
It was a long, weary, dry spell without our quiet time.
Without the daily influence of Your presence,
without drinking daily from the well of Living Water,
I was becoming spiritually dehydrated.
Dangerously so.
All the more dangerous
because I didn't realize how bad it had become.

I was lulled into apathy by the enemy.
But I allowed it.

Please forgive me, Lord,
for You are my First and True Love.

It is at times like this that I begin to understand King David better.
How he could love You so much...
Fighting giants with the faith of a child.
Writing beautiful poetry to honor You.
And then just...

...wander away from You.

Doing things that were spiritually inappropriate. [24]
Living as if You had done nothing for him.
As if you meant nothing to him.

Thank You for the soul-deep lesson, Lord.
Thank You for drawing me back in spite of my disobedience
and for rescuing me from myself.
Again.

In Your gracious Name I pray...
Amen.

Thank You

Thank You, beloved Savior.
For being here in the good times and the bad.
For nudges from Your Spirit and reminders of Your Presence.

For blowing on the spark in my soul
and rekindling the embers that lie within.

For the palpable difference You make in my life.
For the gentle whisper of Your Spirit
telling me how much You love me.
For being a King that longs to have a personal relationship with me,
Your lowliest servant.

For Your call to draw closer to You in times of stress,
that You may comfort and guide me.
For Your compassionate understanding
when I begin to go beneath the waves.
For the grasp of Your hand pulling me back up again.
And again. And again.
For being with me regardless of what I'm going through.
For always being just a whisper away.

For loving me not just in spite of my humanity
but because of it.

For grace, mercy, peace, love and forgiveness.
For the Holy Spirit's still, small voice.
For the peace that passes all understanding.
For being the Voice of Truth.
For undoing me with Your love, compassion, and majesty.
For being more God than I could possibly imagine.
For the beauty in Your creation.

For the beauty that is You.

Part Six:
Love Letters
From God

"You are living so small.
I want to give you life, and that
extravagantly, in Me..."
~ "Living Small"

I See All of You

God:
Where are you?

Me:
I'm right here, Lord.

God:
Are you? You've been avoiding Me, child. Why?

Me:
I'm not sure, Lord. Maybe fear. Selfishness.
A deep unwillingness to give complete control over to You.
Or, rather, fear of what that would look like for my life.
That I wouldn't be the one in control. Search my heart, Lord. Please help me.
Tell me what You see. Because my spirit wants to live for, worship, praise,
and honor You, but my flesh has other ideas. Please tell me what You see and
strengthen my resolve and follow-through, that I may live for You.

God:
I see you. Every part of you.

I see a child who loves Me more than she can express, but who wanders away
from Me for days at a time. Or longer.

I see a follower who would give everything she owns to be with Me but who
holds "things" so closely that they are borderline false idols...all while she
agonizes over letting go of "things" to further My cause.

I see a daughter who draws closer to Me, seeking to hear My heartbeat, but
who sometimes draws away in restlessness, discomfort, and discontent when
she hears it.

I see a branch who desires to bend to My will in the storms of life but who
guards herself so she doesn't bend too far.

I see clay eager to be molded by her Potter but loathe to go through the necessary process to become My masterpiece.

I see a bond-servant eager to please her Master but not doing what He asks.

I see a writer given a gift to share with others but who guards that gift out of fear and selfishness.

I see a wife, mother and grandmother who aches for the salvation of her loved ones, who longs to teach future generations about Me, but who doesn't always lead by example.

I see a steward who yearns to be faithful but who is mishandling My resources.

I see the disciple you could be if you chose to fully trust Me and I see the souls and opportunities lost when you don't.

I see you.
Every part of you.

I see My child, living in a fallen world but still persevering for Me.

I see one of My sheep, once lost and now found.

I see My righteousness, not your filthy rags.

I see My light in you, burning brightly in the darkness that surrounds you.

I love you in spite of all your faults; in spite of all your failures.
Of course I want you to do your best for Me...I expect no less.
But I will never cease loving you because you stumble and fall.
I will help you back up, brush you off,
and continue on the journey with you.

So take My hand, child, and follow Me closely.
You are forever Mine.

Let the Healer Set You Free

'And I will open up my heart and let the Healer set me free...' [25.]
My child,
you sing of opening your heart and letting the Healer set you free,
but is that what you are truly doing?

Even now there are parts of your heart that you reserve for yourself
and don't allow Me free access.
Like a disease, the darkness will creep back out of its boundaries
until it spills over into all areas of your life.

Allowing these tainted areas of your heart to continue on
is like trying to sleep in a bed in which foxtails have been scattered.
You may lay down in that bed, thinking you will be able to rest,
but the reality will soon become self-evident.
The rest that you thought you were going to get will be interrupted
by uncomfortable reminders that your lack of due diligence
has caused you pain, suffering, irritation, and unrest.
And until you get up and clean it up,
your attempts at true rest will be compromised.

You are no different.

When you do not allow Me complete access to your heart and soul
you will find you cannot completely rest in Me,
as if a spiritual foxtail is trying to burrow its way into your heart.
Those uncomfortable reminders
will cause you pain, suffering, irritation, and unrest
until you choose to throw open the doors of your heart and soul
and allow Me free access to clean house.

Open up your heart and let the Healer *truly* set you free!

Breaking Free

Now dimly...then face-to-face. Now in part...then fully.[26.]
My child, I see your heart.
I see your desire to serve and honor Me in your sin-stained world.

I see your decision to break free of the shell
that has confined you up to this point.
Like a bird breaking out of its shell,
you lay in My hand afterward, exhausted,
panting from the exertion of a struggle of epic proportions,
freed in ways you cannot yet comprehend.

I see your faith.
I see the gifts I gave you blooming like the simplest of daisies,
yet perfumed with a scent that pleases Me more
than the most exotic blooms.

I see your joy.
I see the tears you cry when my Spirit overwhelms
your soul past the point of words.

I see the ache in your soul
to be My faithful bond-servant despite the cost.

I see you, My child,
and one day soon your soul will break free
of the bonds of earth
and you will see Me...
face-to-face.

Beautiful

They say 'Beauty is in the eye of the beholder.'
What beauty do You see when You look at me, Lord?
What do You see that makes you smile and look again?
How am I beautiful to You?

When your smile, bubbling forth from the inside out, reaches your eyes. Your love for Me. Your willingness to be transparent and let others see how I rescued you, and how I've been working in your life. The way you delight in the simplicity and beauty of a simple dandelion, and how you are completely undone when I draw near to you. Your willingness to put your ear to the post and become My bond-servant. Your longing to be Home with Me, all while desiring to remain here that you may do My will. That you know you are doing My will imperfectly, yet you keep trying. How you close your eyes and tilt your head as you listen for My voice. Your willingness to let Me mold and shape you even though it's not always comfortable, and even knowing that you will go through more trials by fire before you will be most useful. My Spirit residing in you.

The enemy, and the world through him, would have you believe that I didn't know what I was doing when I created you. That somehow I made a mistake. On the contrary, My child, I knew precisely what I was doing when I formed you. I don't expect perfection from you. Why do you expect it from yourself? Just keep doing your best while you lean on Me, and continue to seek My will and wisdom. You are beautiful to Me, child.

You always have been. And you always will be.

Heavenly Finances

My child,
The resources I have entrusted to you are not yours, but Mine. And when you fritter them away, or lackadaisically pay bills, thereby incurring penalty charges or interest, you are not just misusing My resources. You are misusing the resources I would have used to save other souls from the enemy. By ignoring your responsibilities, you are unknowingly aiding and abetting his plans. The money spent on fines and late fees is money that could be used to further My plans. My money, My plans. Open your eyes, child, and see how your selfishness, laziness, and apathy are having eternal ramifications. Not just for you, but for others. You say you love Me with all your heart, but what fruit are you bearing? Fruit of My Spirit? Or the enemy's?

Beloved Lord,
please help me to be a good steward,
financially responsible with what You have entrusted to me.
My spirit knows the truth, but my flesh is duplicitous.
I freely hand it all over to You, Lord,
and I plea for Your forgiveness and Your help.

I cannot control it
and I do not want it controlling me.

Help me be the steward You created me to be.
The steward You want me to be.
The steward I long to be.

Teach me to walk in Your ways,
and to bear the fruit of Your Spirit,
that I may honor You in all that I say and do.
For You are gracious, merciful,
and mighty in all of Your ways.

All of this I pray in Your precious and holy Name...
Amen.

The Time is Near

Why is it, Lord, though I know how truly good, kind, loving,
merciful, compassionate, and forgiving You are,
that there are times I wander away from You?
The enemy's ploys, yes, but...
Why, when I have been the recipient of such love, when things are going
truly well between You and me, do I just wander off?!?

My child, you so easily say, "The enemy's ploys, yes, but..." with no true knowledge of how much that enemy hates Me and, by association, you and the rest of mankind. He will do and use anything at his disposal to try to defeat Me, and to separate Me from those I ransomed from hell.

Think about everything he orchestrated to try to kill Me. It was a futile effort, as I already knew his intent and was using it as part of My own plan to rescue mankind. But if he was willing to go to that much trouble, why do you naively think, "Yes, the enemy's ploys, but...?" Why? Because he wants you to dismiss him as ineffective.

Has he already been beaten? Yes! In ways he cannot yet comprehend. He knows he lost a huge battle with me, but he refuses to acknowledge he's lost the war. So he is trying to take as many as he can with him into the pit of hell on the final day.

I gave you the gift of faith, as well other gifts. The enemy knows of your love for Me, and your desire to serve Me. He knows he cannot attack your love for Me or your faith in Me, so he distracts you. He tempts you with an air of complacency, trying to convince you that there is plenty of time. Sometimes it works.

And then I waken you, once again, from your spiritual slumber. For there is an eternal urgency at stake...that of the souls yet unsaved. Those still in danger of being carried to the pit of hell at the end of days.

So stay awake. Do not slumber. Pray with me. For the time is near.

Awakening From Slumber

My child, as you keep stirring from slumber,
seeking to shake off the lethargy that tries to pull you back down,
seeking to focus on Me and what I have planned for your life,
so I see your soul stirring and awakening from a long slumber.

I created you, My child.
My eyes beheld you before you even existed.
I formed and knitted you together in your mother's womb. [27.]
I know you intimately.
From before your birth to the moment
when you will come Home to be with Me,
there is no one that knows you better than I do.
Even yourself.

So bear that in mind when I say that I've been waiting
for a very long time for you to awaken from this spiritual slumber.
Waiting for you to wake up and shake off the grip the enemy has had on you.
You are Mine, and you will be forever.
Nothing can change that.

You have no idea the joy and delight I get when you
actively seek My heart and My presence.
It is the reason I stepped out of My judge's robes
and paid your ransom with My own life.
I've wanted to be in relation with you since before time began.
I've wanted you to find peace. My peace.
And hope. My hope.
The joy that comes with finding them has been like a balm on your soul.
The smile on your face and the overflowing joy in your soul
delight me to no end, My child.
One day, sooner than you know, we will see each other face-to-face
and you will see My delight in person.
Until then you can only imagine the joy I feel
as your soul stirs and awakens from slumber.

127

Living Small

You are living so small.

I want to give you life,
and that extravagantly,
in Me.

By hemming yourself into human boundaries
you limit yourself in ways that are not Mine,
for I have no such limitations.

I long to show you the plans I have for your life
but your eyes are focused on what you can do,
not what I can do.

In doing so,
you miss the joy of the life I planned for you
before you were even born.

The world's path is divergent from Mine.
Neither near nor parallel,
it is completely divergent from My plan for your life.

The life that I planned for you,
along with its joy and contentment,
is on My path.

The choices you make will only take you on only one of two paths:
Mine or the world's.

Which one shall it be?

Deepest Recesses

You lift your hands up to Me in praise and worship
yet you have not given yourself over to Me completely.
I know that you love Me, and you long to do what I ask,
but you reserve a corner of your life for yourself.

By doing so you tacitly allow the enemy to take control
of that portion of your life and banish Me from entering within.
Whether that is your intent or not, that is what occurs.
The darkness of the enemy festers in that part of your life.

But the enemy is not content to stay there.

Instead, he will spill over into other sections of your life
that you have reserved for Me,
thereby tainting them
and causing distance between you and Me.

I want to come into the deepest recesses of your heart
and bring new Life to them.
I am not content, anymore than the enemy is,
with being confined to a portion of your life.
I want My Spirit to spill over into all areas of your life,
without reservation, for My glory.

I don't want others to look at you and see
either your image or that of the enemy.
I want them to see My image
and give glory, worship and praise to My Father in Heaven.

So when you lift your hands and heart up in praise and worship,
open up all parts of yourself to Me.

Especially the parts
you've reserved for yourself.

I See You

I see you.

I see you...
even when you think I'm not watching.

I see your hurt...
even when you do your best to hide it.

I see your tears...
even when you're not crying.

I see your anger at your helplessness...
and your inability to change the past.

I see your desire to control everything in your life...
to make up for that which you could not control.

I see your sadness...
the empty, aching void that threatens to swallow you whole.

I see you juggling so much...
partly to take care of business,
partly to prove that you can,
and partly to silence your thoughts.

I see your confusion...
trying to make sense of a senseless situation.

I see your love...
buried deep beneath your cares and worries, but always there.

I see you.

What do you see?

Part Seven: Warfare

"Lord Jesus, this is a battle that begins
in the spiritual realm. I ask for
Your intervention and guidance...."
~ *"Never Enough"*

Never Enough

We've been down this road before, haven't we, Lord?

The times I've quietly closed the door when You knocked
because I was afraid.
Afraid of accepting the responsibilities You were giving me.
Afraid of letting You down.
Afraid I wasn't "enough".

But the ironic thing is that I will never be "enough".
Ever.

The sooner I fully accept that fact the better off I will be.
Because while I am not and never will be "enough,"
You are!

You neither expect nor desire me to go through this life
under my own power.

So why do I expect it of myself?

Why do I keep trying to survive on the power of a faulty 9 volt battery
when I could tap into the Eternal power of the Son?!?

Is my current situation greater than You?
No!

Is my fear greater than You?
No!

Does the enemy revel when I am crippled by fear?
Yes!

Does my fear serve any purpose other than to cripple me?
Yes!

Are there tasks You ask of me that aren't being accomplished
because of this fear?
Yes!

Does the enemy quake, tremble, and rage when I am freed,
by and in You, from this fear?
Yes!

Do I long to be a faithful, trustworthy bond-servant
who implicitly trusts You and does Your will to the best of her ability,
understanding fully that my strength is not my own, but my Master's?
Yes, yes, and yes!!!

Lord Jesus, this is a battle that begins in the spiritual realm. [28.]
I ask for Your intervention and guidance.
For it wasn't a spirit of fear that You gave me [29.]
but one of power, love, and self-control.

Help me to remember that You are greater than anything I will ever face. [30.]
Ever.

I put on the spiritual armor You have given me, my Lord: [31.]
the belt of truth, the breastplate of righteousness, the gospel of peace,
the shield of faith, the helmet of salvation,
and the sword of the Spirit, which is the Word of God.

I choose to take a step of faith, Lord,
clad with Your Heavenly armor,
knowing that You are standing right by my side.

Because while I am not "enough"
and never will be,
You always have been.
And You always will be. [32.]

In Your glorious, righteous, mighty Name I pray...
Amen.

Doing Battle

Lord Jesus, please forgive me for my actions.

I let my human nature take over and found myself
angry, frustrated, and full of self-condemnation.
I allowed it to spill over onto my family because I was being selfish
and focusing on my own problems.

And then the mouth.

Words that I haven't said in a long time, and didn't miss,
spewing forth and poisoning the air.

Please forgive me, Lord.

Help me.
Please.
To stay on Your Path even when things go wrong.
To remember to draw close to You.
To cling to Your side when the enemy
throws trials and temptations at me.
To call him and his minions out
for the liars and unclean lot that they are.
To stand strong in Your strength, not my own,
for my strength is as feeble as a babe in arms.

In the Name of Jesus Christ
I pray a hedge of protection around this house
and those who enter herein.

In the Name of Jesus Christ
I pray for as many angelic warriors as are needed
to surround and protect us from satan's ploys.
To help us fight the battle.
To open our eyes to the deceptions of the enemy.

In the Name of Jesus Christ
I rebuke and command to silence
the spirits of anger, frustration, self-condemnation,
vulgarity, depression, anxiety, doubt, fear,
bickering, idolatry, self-pity, pain, impatience,
superiority, drugs, poor health,
and any other unclean spirits
that were not mentioned by name.

In the Name of Jesus Christ I bind these unclean spirits
with the strongest ties available,
cast them into the deepest part of hell,
and command them to stay there and not return!
They are not welcome here!

And in the Name of Jesus Christ
I pray in their place
the fruits of the Holy Spirit:
love, joy, peace, patience, kindness, goodness,
faithfulness, gentleness and self-control.

I choose the way of the Holy Spirit in which to walk,
not that of the enemy.

I choose to crucify my sinful nature
and follow my Lord and Master wherever He may lead.

I choose to live by and keep step with the Holy Spirit
despite the flesh's desire to the contrary.

I choose Jesus.

All of this I pray in the precious,
glorious, mighty and matchless
Name of Jesus Christ,
my eternal Lord and Savior...
Amen.

Armed for Battle

Lord Jesus, I claim and put on the full armor that You gave me[33.]
knowing that You paid, in full, the ultimate price for my protection
and that there is no better protection available at any price.

I don the breastplate of righteousness
knowing that my heart and soul are my center mass,
that they are where the enemy would shoot to kill,
and that I need to protect them
for they belong to You.

I tie on the belt of truth
knowing that Your truth wraps around me,
girds me, strengthens me,
and holds everything in its proper place.

My feet are shod with the readiness from the Gospel of peace
knowing that the message of good news that You entrusted to me
was meant to be shared with others, journeying far and wide,
not stagnating in one place without bearing fruit.

I firmly grasp my shield of faith
knowing that it will deflect the fiery darts of the enemy
as long as I use it as it was intended
and never lay it where the enemy could steal it.

I strap on my helmet of salvation
knowing that it will protect me from
the fatal blows of discouragement and doubt
that the enemy will try to inflict.

I carry the sword of the Spirit, the Word of God,
knowing that I may need it at a moment's notice
to cut a swath through satan's dominion of darkness
and bring light to a darkened soul.

Sharper than any two-edged sword,
I carry it close to hand and at the ready.

Thank You, Lord Jesus, for the full suit of armor
that You have provided for me.
Help me to wear it at all times.

All for,
and because of,
Your eternal, matchless glory.

In Your righteous, holy, and majestic Name I pray...
Amen.

Stewardship of Time

Lord Jesus,
I love You and long to serve You.
You are my Rock, Foundation, Savior, and One True Love.
Search my heart, O Lord, and know that all of this is true.

And yet...

My traitorous flesh seeks solace in other distractions.
Distractions put in place by the enemy with the intent
of usurping Your rightful place in my heart and soul.

You have been opening my eyes to these forms of idolatry in my life.
Be they games on my phone,
time spent on social media,
or watching television...
minutes, hours and days
have been whittled away.
For nothing.

How many years of my life have been spent on these distractions?

I lay these false idols on the altar of my heart and soul, Lord,
and I offer them up to You.

Thank You for opening my eyes to their insidious ways.
I seek Your wisdom and strength in banishing their influence.
Help me to be a faithful steward with the time You have given me.

In Your gracious and faithful Name I pray...
Amen.

Releasing This Burden

Help me to resolve the frustration and anger I feel, Lord.
It's wearing on my spirit.

I know I'm not guiltless.
I know I have faults.
I know that I am not an exemplary parent,
spouse, or even human being.

I know that I have a lot of room to grow in You
and that I will continue growing until the moment I arrive Home.

I know that I want to honor You above all.
And I know that hanging onto this burden is anything
but honoring to You.

So I release it into Your very capable hands and pray,
in Your Name, for a hedge of protection.
Send angelic warriors to fight this battle, my Lord.
I seek all power in Heaven
because this is not just a battle of human wills...
it begins in the spiritual realm.

Lord, I release this burden to You
and I ask for Your guidance in what steps I should take.
Lead me on Your path,
that I may honor You in all that I say and do.

In Your mighty and righteous Name I pray...
Amen.

Intercession For Loved Ones

Lord Jesus,
I come before You to plea for my loved ones.
My heart aches for the hurt and pain they are going through
and the fallout it is creating in their lives.

Merciful Lord, please heal their broken hearts.
Wash over them with Your balm of peace
and let them feel enclosed in Your arms,
as if they've been gently wrapped in a comforter.

I know You never intended this for them;
this is from the enemy.
I also know, Lord, that You can turn
what the enemy intended for evil into good.
Greater is He who is in me than he who is in the world!
I claim these promises for my precious loved ones.

In Your righteous, holy, and mighty Name,
I pray a hedge of protection around them.
Send as many angelic warriors as are needed to fight this battle.
Position angelic warriors, for each one, as spiritual bodyguards.

Lord Jesus, those lackeys of the enemy...
the voices of fear and grief that are tearing them apart...
shut their mouths and do not allow them
to torment my loved ones further.

I pray instead that You will give them respite in their journey
and help them to feel the nearness of Your sweet Presence.
Help them to rest gently in the palm of Your hand
as they trust that You will be their Comforter.

In Your mighty, righteous, and holy Name I pray...
Amen.

Seeking Heavenly Coverage

Lord Jesus,
I lift up this day and ask
for Your coverage.

Not because of anything in particular
but everything in general.

In Your precious and holy Name I pray
a hedge of protection around this day.

Send angelic warriors to help combat
anything and everything the enemy may send
in his attempt to make me stray from Your path.

You are mighty and merciful in all Your ways,
and I seek Your guidance for this
and every other
day of my life.

In Your beloved Name I pray...
Amen.

Stewardship

Lord Jesus, please help me to give everything I own
back over to You.

It's not truly mine, anyway...it's Yours.
You are simply entrusting me with Your resources for a time.

I want to be a trustworthy steward for You.
Search my heart...
You know I do.

And yet, like Peter denying You three times, [34.]
there are times I let my all-too-human side take charge.
The spirit is willing, but the flesh is traitorous.

What I allow to blossom and bear fruit in my heart and soul
is what I proclaim to be of first importance in my life.

I want You to be first, Lord, not me.
You and Your Way are of the utmost importance.

I want the fruit of Your Spirit to blossom exponentially in my life.
Every area, every corner, every stronghold.

I long for my life to be a pleasing gift to You.
I ache to honor You in all that I do.

Please help me.

Send angelic warriors to help fight this battle,
for this servant girl knows both her own weaknesses
as well as Your matchless strength.
And that with You anything is possible.

Even this.

Sacrificing Idols

Lord God,
I lift up the false idols in my life and give them to You.

Whether people, things, or ideals,
give me strength, wisdom, and peace
to release to You anything...
...*anything*...
that I put in Your rightful place. [35.]

I place them on the altar of my heart and soul
and I sacrifice them to You.

For You alone are the True, Living God.
You alone have the true answers to my questions.
You alone are the Creator and Master of my soul.
You alone are worthy of all glory, worship, and praise.

Please forgive me for betraying You with false idols.
Thank You for Your faithfulness even when I am faithless.

Help me, Lord.
To continue surrendering to You in all areas of my life.
To recognize when I commit idolatry.
To listen for Your still small voice.
To clear my heart of issues that can bog it down.
To accept personal responsibility for my actions and reactions.
To find my eternal hope in You.
To live only for You and for Your glory,
that Your Name may be lifted high.

Now and forevermore.

Part Eight:
This Doesn't Have To
Be The End

"He longs for you to draw close to Him.
He knows you better than you know yourself
and still He loves you..."

~ *"Do You Long to Yadá Jesus*
Christ?"

Do You Long to Yadá Jesus Christ?

If you have...
~ Never accepted Jesus Christ as your Lord and Savior, but you are feeling pulled to turn your life over to Him...
~ Accepted Christ as your Lord and Savior, but have wandered so far away from His loving arms that you're not sure if He'll welcome you back...
~ Accepted Christ as your Lord and Savior, but you aren't living like it...
~ Been reading these poems, prayers, and devotionals, and long to have a living, personal relationship with Jesus Christ but you don't know how...

Know that...
~ Sins are the wrong things you do that would separate you from God.
~ Everyone has sinned and fallen short of the glory of God. No exceptions.
~ He loves you more than you can possibly imagine or fathom, and He longs for you to draw close to Him.
~ He knows you better than you know yourself and *still* He loves you. *Still* He longs for you to draw near.
~ His love for you exceeds the love of all others. No one else can come close.
~ Jesus loves you so much that He died to pay for the debt of your sins.
~ Jesus died on the cross, but He rose again from the dead and is alive in Heaven.
~ If you sincerely confess your sins and ask Him for forgiveness, asking Him to be your Lord and Savior, He will wash your sins away and you will be saved.
~ All who accept Jesus Christ as their Lord and Savior become adopted into His family.
~ It's not too late for you. You've never committed a sin He can't forgive. But now is the time to seek Him. Your next breath isn't guaranteed.
~ Prayer is just talking to God. Nothing more, nothing less. He'll always listen.

If you aren't sure what to pray to ask Him to be your Lord and Savior, here is a sample prayer that you can pray. It doesn't have to be word-for-word...it's just a starting point:

Thank you for loving me, Lord Jesus, even though I am a sinner. I know I have done things that were wrong, things that would cause me be to be separated from You for all of eternity. I'm sorry for my sins. I believe that you are the Son of God, and that You died on the cross to take my punishment. Please forgive me of all of my sins, and wash my heart and soul clean. I accept You as my Savior. Please come into my life and help me turn away from sin. Thank You for forgiving me. Thank you for allowing me to have a personal relationship with You, both now and for all of eternity. Thank You for the day that I will see You face-to-face in Heaven. Help me to live for You, every day, for the rest of my life.

In Jesus' holy, righteous Name I pray...Amen.

If you sincerely prayed that or a similar prayer, then Jesus Christ has come into your heart and soul and made you a new creation. You are now part of His family and a child of God. His Holy Spirit now resides in your heart, helping you to live for Him.

Take the time to get to know Jesus, the One Who saved you. Spend time praying, reading the Bible, and obeying Him. Try not to sin again, but if you do (we all do it...we're human, after all!), talk to God about it. Salvation isn't something that you can lose because you sin again, but that doesn't mean you should sin just because you can. Ask Him for His forgiveness and to help you not sin. He knows what's truly in your heart. He knows if you are trying to follow His guidance...or if you're just shining Him on.

Get a notebook, or a blank book, and journal about your relationship with this precious Savior of yours. It can be as simple or as extensive as you like. Write down prayer requests, and answers to those prayer requests. Journal the things you feel Him putting on your heart. Take the time to study the Bible to see if it lines up with what you're feeling. If you aren't sure if what you are hearing is coming from Him, know that He will never contradict what is in the Bible. Pray and ask Him for understanding and clarification so that you can follow in His footsteps.

Welcome (or welcome back) to the family, brother- or sister-in-Christ! Know that you are loved, and that you have been prayed for before, during, and after the publication of this book. May God bless you abundantly in all that you do for Him. I look forward to meeting you one day, in Heaven if not here on earth.

In Christ's love,
Kristine Bidne

About the Author

Kristine Bidne is a complex person.

Daughter. Sister. Wife. Mother. Grandmother.

Cook. Cashier. Photographer. Author.

Bibliophile. Logophile. Theophile.

Extroverted. Introverted.

Nerd.

Lost. Found.

Sinner. Forgiven.

Orphaned. Adopted.

Child of the One True King.

Grateful.

Index

Notes

1. Pronounced yaw-dah'.
2. 1 Corinthians 13:12
3. John 3:14-18; Galatians 2:20b; John 15:12-13
4. Luke15:11-24
5. 2 Timothy 2:13
6. John 14:15-21
7. Hebrews 13:15
8. Matthew 16:13-7
9. Isaiah 55:8-9
10. Psalm139:7-12; Romans 8:31-39
11. 1 John 5:14-15; Matthew 7:9-11
12. Ephesians 2:4-10
13. Matthew 9:10-13
14. 1 John 1:9-9
15. Romans 3:23
16. Isaiah 55:8-9
17. Luke 15:11-32
18. Psalm 42:1
19. Psalm 139:23-24
20. Matthew 6:27
21. Matthew 25:23
22. Isaiah 55:6
23. Luke 17:11-19
24. 2 Samuel 11:1-27
25. "I Could Sing of Your Love Forever" by Martin Smith.
26. 1 Corinthians 13:12-13
27. Psalm 139:13-16
28. Ephesians 6:10-18; 2 Timothy 1:7
29. 2 Timothy 1:7
30. 1 John 4:4
31. Ephesians 6:10-17
32. Revelation 22:13
33. Ephesians 6:10-17
34. Matthew 26:31-35; Matthew 26:69-75
35. Exodus 20:3-5